400 BROTHERS AND SISTERS

Their Story Continues...

Judy Gordon

Author of *Four Hundred Brothers and Sisters: The Story of Two Jewish Orphanages in Montreal, Quebec, 1909–1942*

To Alexander Rogovsky Kostman –
Your family is well represented –
Enjoy the memories –
Judy Gordon
Sept 2004

MJ PUBLICATIONS

Canadian Cataloguing in Publication Data
Gordon, Judy, 1935–
400 Brothers and Sisters: Their Story Continues . . .
Includes Index.

ISBN: 0-9734254-0-7

The publisher would like to acknowledge the use of images provided by the National Archives of the Canadian Jewish Congress, Montreal, and the Jewish Public Library Archives, Montreal.

Cover photo by Rick Midanik, copyrighted by the *Toronto Star*
The alumni's 1989 reunion—(top row) Sophie Feldman Kazdan, Herb Rasminsky, Sylvia and Sam Rasminsky, Earl Greenberg; (front row) Myer Gordon.

Editing by Andrea Lemieux Editing Services
Electronic formatting by Heidy Lawrance Associates
Illustration by Ernest Raab (1926–2003)

Published by
MJ Publications
14 Alonzo Road
Toronto, ON
Canada M2R 1T5

Illustration by Ernest Raab
(1926–2003)

Dedicated
to
my dear Myer,
Montefiore Home resident, 1926–1936;

- to -
Eiran Harris, archivist, Jewish Public Library, Montreal,
for his most gracious assistance in sending us all
the latest *old* illustrations and anecdotes
which help bring alive this special history;

and

to the
MHOH alumni,
whose heartwarming story is being told
to a community that is finally listening.

CONTENTS

LIST OF ILLUSTRATIONS

FOREWORD

This book brings to light again the true story of the remarkable unsung heroes of the Jewish community who worked so hard and tirelessly to look after children in need.

Because these were the years before miracle drugs and health benefits, many a parent succumbed to an early demise, creating untold hardships for the remaining parent, and of course, the children.

The tradition of caring and compassion is well documented here, and makes one very proud of one's heritage.

The stories gleaned from still more *brothers and sisters* reinforces the fact that this was a positive and rewarding experience for them—for the most part.

This was a world everyone should know about—to be understood and appreciated—because it has brought us, as individuals and a modern Jewish community, to where we are today.

Sandy and Earl (Montefiore Home alumnus) Greenberg

PREFACE

Eleanor Roosevelt once wrote, "Many people will walk in and out of your life, but only true friends will leave footprints in your heart."

How else to explain the bond between the girls and boys of Montreal's two Jewish orphanages—a bond that spans more than sixty years, and has not lessened but remains constant.

Since the first writing of *Four Hundred Brothers and Sisters*, new information has surfaced—more history, more live stories, more photos, more biographies, and more anecdotes. People phoning to say they think they, or their family members, were in one of the homes, or volunteered there. They wanted to share, and be told about the homes, the children.

All these personal stories from the past reveal that life in the orphanages takes on real meaning these many years later; the memories of the lives these real children experienced as residents have sustained them through their years as alumni.

For instance, Sara Frenkel, a Montreal Home alumna now living in Toronto, got so excited upon seeing our book, and then, she cried out in shock when looking closely at the cover photo where she discovered her aunt and uncle, Esther and Daniel Cohen, among the adults on the back porch of the summer camp main house! Her comment: "How sad that there is no one left to show it to and even tell."

Connie Rosen, daughter of the late Tina Wiseman Rosen, posed this interesting question: "If there are four hundred brothers and sisters, does that make you [the spouses], and the rest, my aunts and uncles? And should I expect Hannuka gelt from my four hundred uncles and aunts?"

Other alumni spoke of their fears, sadness, bravery, and the joy—yes, joy—they found in the homes as they struggled to accept why they were there, and to accept eagerly the love and attention they received from a caring staff.

The following article serves to remind readers of what the original *Four Hundred Brothers and Sisters* was about—children who met and became a family while in Montreal's two Jewish orphanages between 1909 and 1942—as written by Montreal *Gazette* reporter Ann McLaughlin in the summer of 1990, following the second MHOH combined reunion.

Whatever became of the underprivileged kids who grew up on the Main during the Depression? Doctors, lawyers, judges, and architects—they told each other yesterday at the forty-eight-year reunion of the Montefiore and Westmount Homes for orphans.

The homes, on Jeanne-Mance Street and Claremont Avenue, took in impoverished or orphaned children of Jewish immigrants who lived between Saint-Lawrence Boulevard and Saint-Denis Street, until closing in the 40s.

Nearly fifty years later, more than 130 people turned up from all parts of the world to swap stories and view tattered photos of the dormitories and camps they shared.

One man in particular was celebrated at the reunion. He was not a resident, but supervised the boys' floors during the mid-1930s. Today, at seventy-eight, he is one of Canada's best known poets—Irving Layton.

"He was a real subversive and taught us to rebel against having to eat oatmeal every morning," joked Irving Pfeffer, then sixty-six and a municipal judge in San Francisco.

"He didn't believe in law, order, and discipline. He was a socialist, I guess, and created some wonderful trouble," said Lester Dick, who went on from the orphanage to become a fashion designer.

Layton said he was fired from the Montreal Home (on Claremont) in 1939 for stirring up too much trouble. "I haven't seen any of these people in almost half a century. I'm really proud tonight. I knew they had it in them."

* * *

Eiran Harris, archivist of Montreal's Jewish Public Library, shared the following: "The two Montreal homes were not unique in the type of guests they welcomed. When the first Jewish orphan home in North America was founded in Charleston, South Carolina, in 1801, the purpose was 'relieving widows, educating, clothing, and maintaining orphans and children of indigent parents.' As you can see, they were not all orphans either."

The orphans written about in this book enjoyed their years in the homes—for the most part. And, as Harris noted when he sent along this story, "Orphans stood, in accordance with Biblical teachings, under the special protection of God. That is why 'it's grand to be an orphan!'" Sholom Aleichem wrote that line in *Adventures of Mottel: The Cantor's Son*, part one: *In Kasrilovka: Hoorah, I'm an Orphan!* The following is excerpted from this piece of literature.

"Mottel was considered an orphan when his father died, even though he still had a mother. He found it to be an advantage, because people took his part in arguments and were punished for making fun of him ... Everybody wanted him—he didn't have to go to school, didn't have to study nor pray, didn't have to sing: 'I'm free of everything.'"

As Harris noted, "The homes did not exist in a vacuum; everyday life went on around them." So, even in the days of Sholom Aleichem, an orphan had one parent, unlike recent years where the connotation is a child without any parents. And did you notice the pride Mottel exhibited in his new status? A bit like the orphans of the Montreal homes when they were fussed over by staff and had many comforts that other children, still at home with their parents, lacked.

The raison d'etre was the same across North America. While there were, eventually, Jewish orphan homes in all major cities during the nineteenth and twentieth centuries, in Canada we are aware only of the two in Winnipeg, one in Toronto (see appendix), and the two in Montreal.

The new information and stories that have made their way to us over the past year and a half show how keen the alumni and their friends are to share their valued memories—to fill the void in Montreal's Jewish history.

We can't pretend there was no such thing as a Jewish orphan, but we *can* be pleased that our community did the right thing at the time, in caring for, and offering love, to a group of children who were in great need. You are greatly appreciated.

We are also very pleased that the Jewish community is now expressing an interest in listening and learning. The new people we have met through this information-gathering process are wonderful and delightful. We are truly blessed.

Judy Gordon
Toronto

NEW KNOWLEDGE FEEDS THE SOUL

The impact of the first book was the revelation to the present community that Jewish orphanages existed in Montreal from 1909 to 1942, and that this information could be used as a definitive history of the homes for years to come.

Considering that the original contained an incomplete history, our hope is to more completely finish the *package* of information and hope that, years down the road, the community will maintain its pride in doing a good—and right—deed.

Information like the following from alumni such as Reva Savitsky Schuman, who was in the Montreal Home in Westmount and who now lives in Tulsa, Oklahoma, came to us.

> While reading the first book, I could better understand when, after leaving the home and arriving at [my mother's poor] flat in the area of Colonial and Duluth, I threw myself on the bed and cried like a baby. However, we all happily survived. I do think that I was born with a sensitivity to my surroundings, and might add that I have always felt that the orphanage has helped shape the kind of person that I am today.

Others are just now remembering that the Montreal orphanages played a role in their family history. Francy Karp, of California, wrote that her mother was in one of the homes.

> I don't have a lot of facts but my grandfather's name was Sidney Lebidensky. He had three daughters: Sarah born about 1902, Fannie born 1903, and my mother, Harriet "Hattie," 1905. My mother's mother died and her father remarried. The custom of the day was that, when the new wife did not want the husband's children, he could put them into an orphanage. That's what happened. An aunt of the sisters brought them to the United States some years later. Their names were Rose and Louie Goldstein. That's what I know for now.

New stories are still coming—one, a 1986 article by Janice Rosen, director, Archives, Canadian Jewish Congress. It appeared in the CJC National Archives newsletter and was based on a collection, donated by Anne Gross, of minute books from the Montreal Hebrew Sheltering and Orphans' Home for the years 1914 to 1922. Also in this collection were annual reports and assorted papers extending through the early 1930s. These documents offer up a fascinating glimpse into Montreal's Jewish community in the early part of the century—and why and how the issue of needy children arose and was taken care of.

In the nineteenth century across Canada, Jewish orphans usually were put into Protestant orphanages, the only ones available. The need for a Jewish-run facility arose because it was against Jewish law to have a Jewish child raised in a gentile home.

When the Baron de Hirsch Institute acquired a building in Montreal in 1892 to shelter immigrants, it also took in homeless children. The home was first located at 507 Saint-Urbain Street, and then moved to 16–18 Evans Street. In 1909, the Montreal Sheltering and Orphans' Home was established to better fill the needs of, and house, orphaned children, the indigent aged, and transients. The term *orphan* was expanded to include children with only one parent, where the remaining guardian was incapable of caring for the child.

The minute books recorded, with consideration, the applications from widows who had no one to care for their children while they worked, and from many destitute fathers whose wives had died from tuberculosis or influenza.

As you read stories from some of these surviving children, you will see that, generally, they were well treated, cared for, and loved by the staff. And they were the envy of the neighbourhood when, every summer, they relocated to a farm in Shawbridge (later called *Sunshine Camp*), where they participated in outdoor activities such as sports, biking, and small-scale farming.

When the orphanage finally moved to 500 Claremont Avenue, the former Hervey Institute, in 1921, the elderly were then housed in separate quarters, which later evolved into the Maimonides Hospital for Geriatric Care.

By the early 1940s, the homes were closed due to a lack of funding and the birth of foster care. There had been two then: the original Montreal Home on Claremont, and the Montefiore Home on Jeanne-Mance, which opened in 1921 as the need to care for more children became apparent. It is through collected records that pieces of this important and unknown part of Montreal's Jewish community's history were filled in.

One of the sources is the National Archives in Ottawa, which has case and subject files of the Montreal Hebrew Orphans' Homes from 1924 to1940. They can be found in the Jewish Family Services section of the Baron de Hirsch Collection.

* * *

Individuals were the beacons of hope for the orphaned children. Charles Soroka is originally from Montreal. His mother-in-law attended one of the Gordons' *reads* and was surprised and excited to find a familiar name in it, that of Charles's great-grandmother, Mrs. D. Slabotsky. She and her husband used to take their children to visit the Montreal Home every second Sunday, bearing gifts and playing with the orphaned kids. "When great-grandfather passed away in 1920," Charles reported, "the visits stopped, but the memories lingered on."

Of all the people who wrote or called the Gordons, some had family in the homes and others were the volunteers who made the homes happier places. Lucy Sadowski wrote,

> Unfortunately, I don't have much detail about my mother's experience in the Montreal Home. It would have been about 1925 plus or minus a couple of years. She and her sister had lost their mother in the big flu epidemic of 1918 and were being cared for by their paternal grandparents. The grandmother was hospitalized, possibly for depression, or a *nervous breakdown*, and the kids had to stay in the orphanage for a while.
>
> My impression was that it was not a very happy experience but not terrible either. I don't know where the orphanage was or what it was called.

* * *

What a small world! While trying to get this book published, public school pals of mine (Judy Gordon) were still surfacing. One of them, Beverlee Freedman Ashmele, heard about Book One through mutual friends and e-mailed me. I soon realized that an Ashmele was mentioned in Book Two and wrote asking if she was related.

Yes! Hattie Ashmele was her late husband's favourite aunt, and, in fact, her son Todd's middle name is Hayes, in her memory.

To recap a bit, in the following Passover story, written in 1916, Hattie was mentioned as being one of the assistants who took excellent care of the children in the Montreal Home. She was born in London, England, in 1890 and came to Canada as a youngster with her married sister. They settled in Montreal, and Hattie had to find a job to help support herself. She found work at the home, still on Evans Street; she was sixteen years old.

Hattie married Myer Kirsch in 1927, as noted in Book One. Also mentioned there was the fact that, when they were courting and Hattie was in the Shawbridge summer camp with her charges, Myer used to walk half the night from his army camp to visit her. Daughter Elma Kirsch Dolansky finds that most amusing. She says her father was never in the army and never liked to walk. But one of his six brothers *was* in the service and later became a general. Two brothers were on the home's board of directors.

Hattie returned to England with Myer to raise their family. During the war, Hattie's youngest son Lionel was reported missing in action and presumed shot down over Germany. The family returned to Canada after the war. Hattie passed away around 1962.

Daughter Elma (to whom we talked for the first time during the editing of Book Two) knows little about her mother's earlier days, but remembers one little story about how one five-year-old orphan, trying to describe her brother's full head of curls, looked up and said, "My brother has one curl."

She also remembers Myer Gordon from the Veterans' Hospital in Sainte-Anne de Bellevue—Myer was in because of ear problems. She was about fourteen, and her father had brought her along with him on one of his visits bringing treats to the patients there. She also remembers Myer from Sherbrooke, Quebec, where her family lived in the late 1940s. The world is truly shrinking.

Passover for *Our* Orphans, 1916-Style

Among other new information received from Eiran Harris was a copy of a continuing series of articles, *Rambles among Our Institutions*, written on April 28, 1916, by Abe Cohen in the *Canadian Jewish Chronicle. Our Orphans' Home* centred on a Passover Seder conducted in the first home. Mention is made as well that across the yard was the original old folks' home; its eight residents, ranging in age from fifty-two to ninety-three, also celebrated with their own Seder.

This event took place in the original orphanage on Evans and Cecil streets, of which we had had practically no information—until now. It gives such a wonderfully magical insight into what Book One tried to impress on its readers—the love and caring received by the children whose unfortunate circumstances caused them to live in the orphanage.

Excerpted here, it is also a fine example of the vernacular of the day, with its quaint sayings, descriptions, and expressions.

> Little Harry Davis and his father, Israel, knocked on the door of the Hebrew Sheltering and Orphans' Home on Evans Street just a few moments after Passover was ushered in on the 14th of Nisan. They asked permission to see the activities of the home on that Seder night. "Let all who are hungry to view our home on this festive night enter and see thereof," was the response of the lady who had answered the door.
>
> And what a sight it was! Gazing inward, Harry saw a spectacle which held him like a spell! The prettiest sight he had ever seen or thought possible ... a sight which "no other Jewish institution or private home in the Dominion could claim as ever having duplicated."
>
> Fifty boys and girls, aged from about three to twelve, were seated around two long, parallel tables. Their eyes were deep blue and *roguish* black; their cheeks brown and rosy; with beautiful and *winsome* faces ... crowned with raven curls and *sun-flouting* hair!
>
> The girls were in velvet dresses, pale pink, white, or blue, with matching bright sashes and dainty ribbons; the boys wore

their neat holiday clothes (not uniforms). All combined to appear as "a great symbol of life in its innocent spring-time."

Harry gazed as if fascinated by some invisible sorcery. To his ears rose the sound of voices from the boys, whose eyes were lifted upward toward a man holding a glass filled with wine ... It was the faith of little children rising up in rapture to heaven visible with blessings.

A milky white tablecloth was adorned with vases of white flowers, bowls of fruit, and plates filled with Passover delicacies "nestled in garden greens." Each child had an Hagadah and a glass of red wine. On the head table rested lighted candles and a Seder plate filled with all the required items to carry out the time-honoured rites of the Seder in the old-fashioned Orthodox style.

Mr. Fisher conducted the symbolic ceremonies, and almost all the children joined in the chanting. Asking the *Fier Kashes* was of great interest to the children, and not one pair of eyes saw Mr. Fisher hide the *Afikomon* under the cushion (at least, that is what he thought!). Maxie Mendelsohn found it almost immediately!

All eyes focused on the open door to welcome in the Prophet Elijah whose full glass of wine awaited, "to refresh him after his long journey through the centuries," whispered one of the older boys. When Elijah failed to arrive, the disappointment was great. One girl reasoned it out that he didn't visit them "through his not caring to soil his white angelic costume while flying over Montreal's dusty streets."

Messrs. A. M. Vineberg and Sol Kellert, president and vice-president of the Sheltering Home, had donated most of the Passover requirements. They felt they could not go home to their own Seders until they had visited the children at the orphanage to watch them at their service. They were so thankful to glance down the long tables at the rows of happy faces. Mr. Vineberg made a short fatherly speech and commended Miss H. M. Armur, superintendent, and her aides, Mrs. Kramer and Miss Hattie Ashmele, for their excellent care and upbringing of the children, obvious for all to see.

The majority of the children were in great need of attention when they came to the orphanage for shelter ... they were "pale-faced and underfed ... it was easily discernible that they were not in that state now; that out of the poor soil of misfortune and poverty something strong and fine and fair was growing."

The farewell greeting of *Happy Yontoff* from the two gentlemen to the children brought the response, "Thank you, Sirs; the same to you!"

The anticipation and preparation for this event brought a great deal of excitement and activity. The boys hovered in the background near the cookery (usually forbidden territory), sniffing the savoury odours and occasionally being permitted to taste some delicacy in the process of being made. The older girls were privileged, and could help sort fruit and prepare the utensils, "being very busy and looking important."

The dishes of victuals were being handed around, and because nearly everyone had (in his or her opinion) contributed something to the feast, either as one of the advanced *nashers* (tasters), sorters of fruit, or *persons of importance*; the supper was peculiarly interesting to the diners who, when they were not eating, beguiled the pauses by remarks, noted by young Harry Davis ... "If these are not good potatoes, I never saw any," observed Miss Soft Voice; "Some of the matsomel that I hear Miss Armur order is in the stuffing of the chicken, that's why it is so nice," said little Dimple Finger; "My dish is swell! Mrs. Kramer told me she never cooked such fresh ones," added Miss White Blouse; "I won some nuts yesterday and placed them in the box with others for Haroseth," was Mr. Cheder-Yingle's little say, and so it went—around the table.

Harry went down to the kitchen—Mrs. Kramer, a pleasant-speaking woman, was in sole charge there, and everything was so spotless that, despite the washing of the dishes and pots used for the Seder, one could have *eaten from the floor*. Six of the oldest girls were instructed daily by Mrs. Kramer in the art of domestic science. (In later years, Mrs. Kramer received many honours from the Board of Directors for her dedicated work at the home, then located on Claremont Avenue in Westmount.)

As Harry was leaving the orphanage, he saw, and heard, Miss Armur pinch the plump cheek of a tot and say, "What is it that makes you so sweet?" The quaint answer was, "I dess when God made me out of dust, He put a little thugar in." Harry complimented Miss Armur for being so well respected and loved by the *inmates*, despite the fact she had only worked there for a few months.

Miss Armur went on to describe her wards as not the orphans, fatherless or motherless, of the rich—those are rarely found in a publicly supported institution. These are the children of the poor, who enter the orphanage half-frightened, a condition brought on by the unfortunate conditions at their former homes. She and her staff treat them as "children who love to play, to whom it is natural that life should seem a merry pastime."

Staff is trained as social workers to understand the needs and interests of the boys and girls. They perform acts of daily, watchful kindness ... to ensure that appropriate words, tones, gestures, and affection are used and maintained, so they are "entirely in sympathy with them."

Miss Armur made some very complimentary references to the Board of Directors of the home, saying, "It is the policy of the men who have made this institution possible, the children be given a home in which they can be taught the few simple things which help to make life less hard on them when they go out to fight the battle in the world. The simple things are honesty, industry, courage, faith in God, in their fellow beings, and themselves."

Harry left the building, walking up Saint-Urbain Street in a dreamlike state, recalling, rehearing, and reliving his evening's experiences: "There stands a haven for God's unfortunate; there stands a beacon-light of hope for our nation; there stands earnestness, sincerity, true education—a genuine wholesome man-in-the-making factor."

Early Archival

The Montefiore Hebrew Orphans' Summer Home in Ste. Agathe, Quebec (1930)
(The cover of the original *Four Hundred Brothers and Sisters*)

Sketch of the Montefiore Home (Originally a church, built in 1909, the dome is being restored to its original beauty)

(Below) Recent photo of the Montefiore Home

CJC National Archives (circa 1920)

Spartak Football Club, runners-up, 1932. This soccer team played in Fletcher's Field, part of the Workers Sport Association (W..S.A.) (Top row) J. Levine (Com), I. Soifer, L. Berman, A. Gammon, S. Mager, A. Shostack, D. Mangel (Sec); (middle row) O. Soiferman, L. Backman, H. Williams, J. Wall (Capt.); (front row) P A. Loss, N. Kozloff, A. Zuker

With thanks to Brian Slepchik, Toronto, for the loan of this photo. His father was a trainer with this team. Photo by Gulkin.

With thanks to Brian

This group of orphans came from Poland in 1918 with Arnold Golub, who was put into the Montefiore Home.

CJC National Archives, Montreal

(Left) A young Hattie Ashmele with some of her charges at the original Montreal Home on Evans Street, circa 1916. Note the uniforms.

(Below centre) An older Hattie at Sunshine Camp, prior to 1927

(Bottom left) Myer & Hattie Kirsch at the wedding of their daughter Elma to Ben Dolansky

(Bottom right) An older, but still pretty, Hattie

The Montefiore Hebrew Orphans' Home

request the presence of you and your friends at the

Annual Passover Provision Shower

on Sunday the Fifteenth of March

nineteen hundred and thirty-one

from 2.30 to 11 p.m.

at

The Home

4650 Jeanne Mance Street

Help to provide for the Orphan and God will help you to provide for your own child

דער מאַנטעפיאָרע בית יתומים

לאדעט איך איין מיט אייערע פריינט צום

יערליכען פסח פראָוויזשאָן שאוער

זונטאָג דעם פופצענטען מארטש, 1931

פון 2.30 ביז 11 אזייגער אין אווענט

אין דער „האָום"

4650 דושין מענס סטריט

העלפט שפייזען דעם יתום, און גאט וועט
איך העלפען שפייזען אייער אייגען קינד

Superintendent and Mrs. Osovsky and children of the Winnipeg Home

The Jewish Orphans' Home, Winnipeg.

Myer Gordon's work permit, issued in 1935, listing his nationality as Jewish, his complexion and eyes—black! A work permit was needed for his outside work as a message boy. The original is now in the CJC National Archives in Montreal.

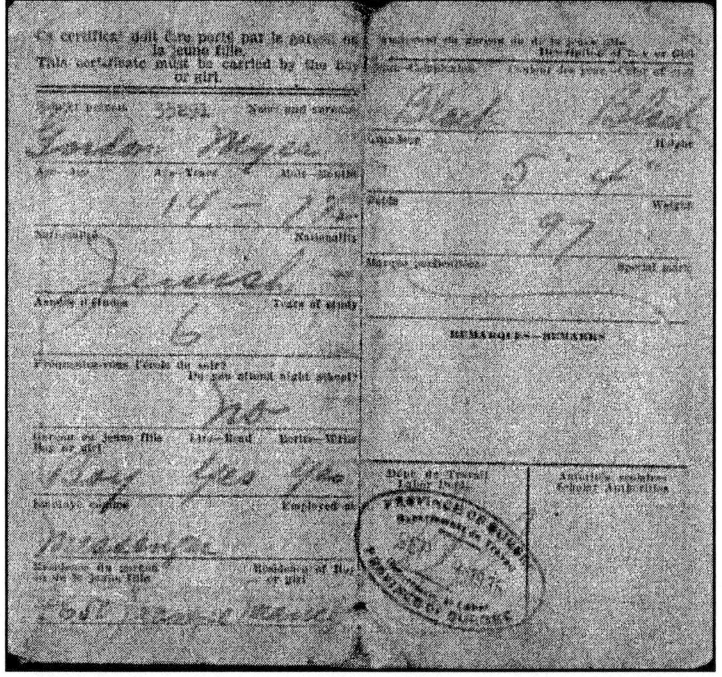

Ce certificat doit être porté par le garçon ou la jeune fille.
This certificate must be carried by the boy or girl.

Gordon Myer

14

Nationality: Jewish

Years of study: 6

Do you attend night school? no

Boy or girl: Boy — Read: yes — Write: yes

Employed at

Residence of boy or girl

Black — Black

Height: 5 4

Weight: 97

REMARQUES—REMARKS

Dépt. du Travail / Labor Dept.

Autorités scolaires / School Authorities

PROVINCE DE QUEBEC

דיזען מאל ווילען מיר בלויז איהר זאלט זיך מיט
אונז מיטפרעהען

מיר האבען ערשט לעצטענס געהאט צוויי בר מצוות פון אונזערע קינדער אין דער הוים, און באלד נאכדעם האבען זיך די סימפאטייזער פון אונזער הוים ווארעם אפגערופען ביים יום טוב שאוער, ווילען מיר יעצט אבסאלוט ניט מאכען קיינע געלט פראפיטען דיזען שבת, שביעי של פסח ביי די בר מצוות פון צוויי פון אונזערע קינדער, און מיר לאדען דעריבער איין אלע סימפאטייזער פון׳ם

מאנטעפיארע בית יתומים

צום דאווענען מארגען שבת, 9 אוהר פריה

אין דער שוהל פון דעם בית יתומים

אום בייצוזיין אהנען די

בר מצוה פון צוויי קינדער

און עס וועט זיין א יום טוב פון בלויז פארגעניגען, אדער בעסער געזאגט, א בלויז גייסטיגען פארגעניגען, אהן וועלכע צוזעקען פאר געלד זאמלונגען.

קומט דעריבער אלע, און נעהמט אנטייל אין דער שמחה

ווייל די קינדער פון מאנטעפיארע בית יתומים דארפען פארעכענט ווערען פאר אונזערע קינדער, און די שמחה דארף דעריבער זיין אונזער שמחה.

מיר מיזען זיין די עלטערען און קרובים צו זייער שמחה.

קומט אלע, מענער און פרויען, מארגען שבת 9 אוהר פריה צום דאווענען

אין האל פון דעם בית יתומים, 4650 מענס סטריט

א. ראגינסקי, טשערמאן הויז קאמיטעט
מ. פעלדמאן, פרעזידענט

This notice invites all supporters of the Montefiore Home to attend a joyous celebration in the home's synagogue to honour the recent bar mitzvahs of two boys from the home. This Saturday morning prayer meeting will create a very happy occasion where everyone can participate and celebrate with the b'nai mitzvahs. From the *Keneder Adler*, April 22, 1924.

Montefiore Hebrew Orphans' Home Outing, (1924) organized by the Raginsky family. Here with some orphans and volunteers.

Photos courtesy of Roslyn Raginsky Liverant

Dance class—Renee Raginsky, age 6, grandchild of Abraham, daughter of Alexander, Shefler's Dance Studio, 1931

Monument in the Shaar Hashomayim Cemetery—"In memory of the children who perished in the fire which destroyed their summer home in Shawbridge August 15, 1922." It is nice to note that people have been visiting; see the stones on the monument.

The names of the children are engraved on the footstone: Louis Spitznick 11 yrs; Joseph Feigelson 8 yrs; Isidor White 9 yrs; Samuel White 7 yrs; Isidor Broitman 7 yrs; Max Broitman 6 yrs; Alfi Schecter 6 yrs; Chona Schecter 5 yrs."

Photos by Harry Pinker, 2004/05/06

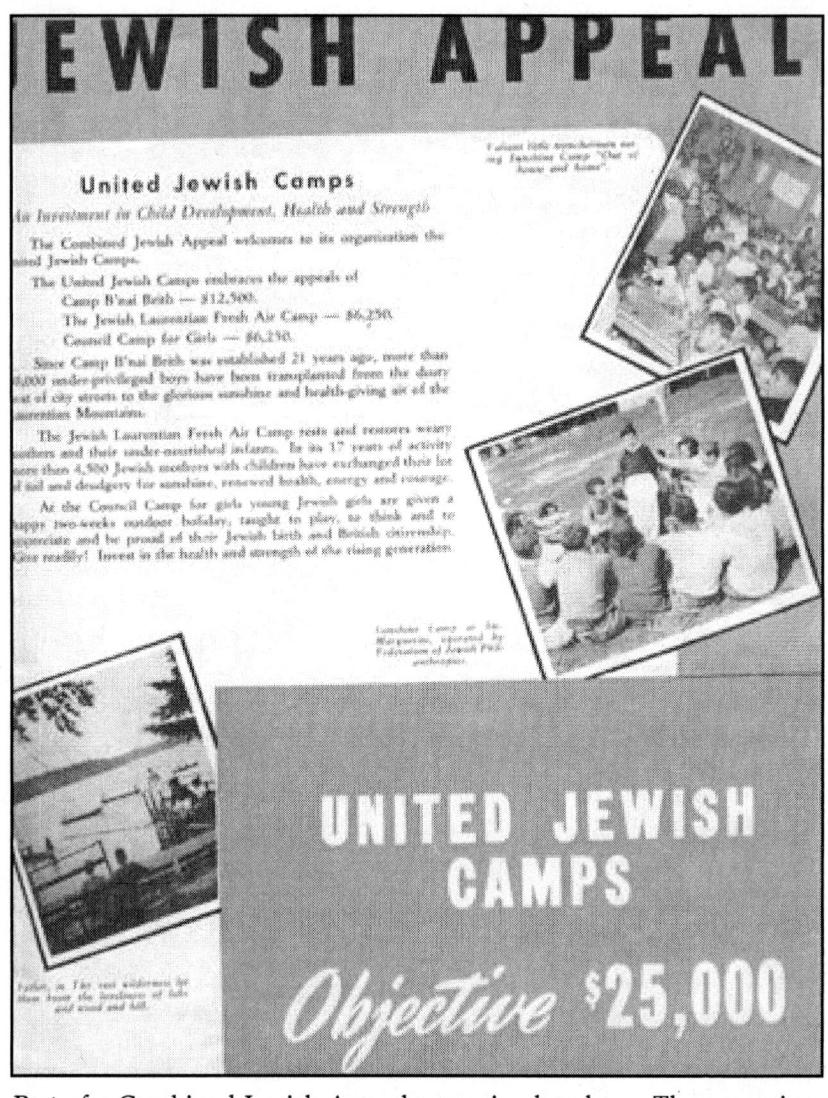

JEWISH APPEAL

United Jewish Camps

An Investment in Child Development, Health and Strength

The Combined Jewish Appeal welcomes to its organization the United Jewish Camps.

The United Jewish Camps embraces the appeals of

Camp B'nai Brith — $12,500.

The Jewish Laurentian Fresh Air Camp — $6,250.

Council Camp for Girls — $6,250.

Since Camp B'nai Brith was established 21 years ago, more than ,000 under-privileged boys have been transplanted from the dusty heat of city streets to the glorious sunshine and health-giving air of the Laurentian Mountains.

The Jewish Laurentian Fresh Air Camp rests and restores weary mothers and their under-nourished infants. In its 17 years of activity more than 4,500 Jewish mothers with children have exchanged their lot of toil and drudgery for sunshine, renewed health, energy and courage.

At the Council Camp for girls young Jewish girls are given a happy two-weeks outdoor holiday, taught to play, to think and to appreciate and be proud of their Jewish birth and British citizenship. Give readily! Invest in the health and strength of the rising generation.

UNITED JEWISH CAMPS

Objective $25,000

Part of a Combined Jewish Appeal campaign brochure. The campaign ran from September 20 to 28, 1943; objective-$583,000. The three photos were taken at the Montreal (Westmount) Hebrew Orphans' Home Sunshine Camp.

Upper right photo: the dining hall. Below that: the main concourse with Phil Adesky standing, Harry Schwartz with his hand on Phil, and counsellor Gerry Waldston seated centre. Bottom left photo: the swimming and boating compound.

The original brochure is still in the hands of alumnus Harvey Israel, Montreal.

Fifty-year contributors (and spouses) to the Combined Jewish Appeal, September 1, 1966.
Dr. A.B. Illievitz, medical director of Montefiore Home in its early years, wearing glasses, is fifth from left, front row.

AN AMAZING YIDDISH TRANSLATION

Other most pertinent new information was received in the spring of 2003—a packet of Yiddish articles published in the *Keneder Adler* in 1931. Eiran Harris discovered that these pertained directly to the two Montreal Hebrew Orphans' Homes and "are a gold mine of information." He further noted that "it is well worth translating ... contains much new information ... There must be someone left in Toronto who is still familiar with Yiddish."

Miriam Beckerman is one of them. She was attending the Association of Jewish Librarians' Conference held in June 2003 in Toronto—as were the Gordons. Because she was busy in the lectures, she agreed to do a *quick read*, and she generously gave of her time to partially and informally translate the seven or so pages.

However, some powers overruled and a complete translation was deemed more appropriate. Montrealer Rebecca Margolis was recommended by Harris, and her word-for-word translation follows.

Please note: Brackets [ ] are used around names for which she was unable to ascertain or verify the spelling or the name, as well as to contain editorial clarification of the original material.

Rebecca noted that the phraseology was at times *flowery* and oftentimes obviously written *of that era.*

The Orphanage in Westmount, M. Ginzburg
Number 11 of the series *Jewish Institutions in Montreal*
July 28, 1931

In the introductory article to this series, we observed that there was initially no separate Jewish orphanage just as there was no separate [Jewish] nursing home. The Jewish settlement was still small and the need was not great enough to create separate organizations like those that exist presently. The building on [Saint-Evan] Street did, although it was not very large, fill the following functions: shelter for the poor, nursing home, and orphanage.

By 1909, the need [within the Jewish community] increased greatly and the number of orphans began to grow. Rather than treating, caring for an orphan on an individual basis, a problem had developed that had to be solved. The first [Jewish] orphanage was established where nine children were taken in from a Protestant home for children. Later, many other Jewish children aged three to nine joined them from a Christian children's organization. For eight years, that is, until 1917, this irregular situation remained.

When the Federation took over the administration of the orphanage in that year [1917], the situation improved greatly. A system was introduced and it became evident that a large independent building had to be established to concentrate more Jewish orphans under one roof. In 1921, the Federation mobilized ... and managed to purchase a five-storey, sturdily constructed building in a remarkably attractive location at 500 Claremont Avenue in Westmount for $100,000. Among the largest donors were Sir Mortimer Davis, Jacob Jacobs, Solomon Kellert, and Ascher Pierce, who each contributed $10,000. There were also donations of $5,000, so that a minimal mortgage remained, which today [1931] does not amount to more than $6,000.

The orphanage remains at that same location in the same building in Westmount, and today there are seventy-two orphans—forty-one boys and thirty-one girls.

At the present moment, thirteen new children are being admitted, two of them of mentally retarded parents who are unable to earn a living. Others are from families where the parents are ill and only able to enter a hospital once they have freed themselves of their children. These fall into the category of *living orphans* [children with living parents] and are raised alongside the actual orphans. Among the new arrivals are also six [children] whom the Federation has billeted in private homes until now. This was particularly expensive for [the Federation]. Of the once sixteen Ukrainian orphans, only three remain. Aside from them, there are also four orphans from Calgary, where there is currently no Jewish orphanage.

The decision to admit a child into the orphanage lies with the Department of Family Welfare, which investigates each case and renders its decision to the orphanage.

The oldest of the children at present is sixteen years old. Ten children in the orphanage are already in high school and six are in business college. The Federation pays an average of $3 a month for each child in high school and between $7 and $12.50 for those in commercial school. Of the older children, four are on the verge of independence, that is, they are employed in various posts and are saving their wages in the bank. It is remarkable how, week in, week out, these children submit their hard-earned wages, which are kept at the bank under their names—with the bankbooks held in the office of the institution.

One girl who is working as a barber has already saved $240 while earning only $10 a week in wages.

A special credit is due the noble Mrs. [Ditenberg] and Mr. A. Greenberg, who have taken a special interest in finding jobs for the older children. There are, incidentally, children here who have been in this institution for more than ten years and have achieved near independence. This is why helping them out with jobs is one of the most important tasks [of the orphanage].

On the Sabbath and Jewish holidays, the children are brought to the Shaar Hashomayim Synagogue to pray. Every day, a minyan [prayer quorum] is held where the older orphans lay tfilin [phylacteries] and pray under the supervision of the assistant superintendent of the institution.

The building is large and there is enough (perhaps even too much) space for the relatively small number of children. In an emergency, the number of children could be doubled. There is a large recreation room, an apothecary, a dental room, a room for the nurse, a special kitchen with an electric stove, fine school rooms, a laundry, library, and so on.

Two special hospital rooms, with ample light and comfort, contain eight beds. The rooms are all spacious, bright, and well equipped. The medical side [of the orphanage] is arranged in the following manner: The medical board, at whose head stands Mr. Bloomberg, consists of twelve doctors, with each doctor working as a volunteer for one month of the year. Dr. Rosenbaum helps those children with eye conditions. Aside from this, a dentist comes in on Sundays to help those with tooth problems.

* * *

Hascal A. Rosen's father was that dentist. Hascal wrote to us out of the blue to say,

> I flipped through the pages [of your book] and came across my late father's name, Dr. Louis Julius Rosen ... he not only spent a good part of each Sunday there offering his time to the residents, but my brother [Seymour] and I vividly recall also that the orphans who were still sitting and waiting for examinations as the *clinic* was closing for the day were told by our father to visit his offices at their convenience. He continued treating them on his own time, never accepting a penny.
>
> I purchased a copy [of your book] and gave it to our mother to read—she was in her ninety-ninth year at that time—and has since passed on. She assisted our father at Claremont Avenue.
>
> My wife, Sandy, and I sponsor a Kiddish at our Sainte-Agathe House of Isreal Congregation once a year in memory of her late father and once a year in memory of mine. In November 2002, when our rabbi asked me to say a few words about mine, I pulled your book from my tallith bag and spoke about my stumbling into the Y ... etc. as mentioned earlier ... Hardly any of the approximately 125 present knew about the orphanages.

Dr. Muriel Gold Poole also wrote to us: "I enjoyed reading it [*Four Hundred Brothers and Sisters*] especially because I grew up in Montreal (same era as you, it seems) and knew nothing about these orphanages."

Muriel's latest book, *Tell Me Why Nights Are Lonesome*, covers some of the same research. "You mentioned my aunt, Rachel Ratner (who assisted the medical staff of the Montreal Home); she was founder of the MDAA (Montreal Dental Assistants Association). There are more details about her in my book and also at CJC, and my father, S. Bernard Haltrecht, was the founding managing director of JIAS (see *The Jew in Canada*, 1926) ... your book is a wonderful contribution to the history of Montreal."

Back to the translation ...

The hygienic side [of things] has also been established at the appropriate level. The children are washed every day. The rooms also indicate order and solid supervision.

It is characteristic for the older children to look after the younger ones and help them with getting dressed, washing themselves, and so on. It is reminiscent of a kind of small *military barracks* where everything goes *by the bell*, strictly and punctually, disciplined and cold.

A girl sleeps in the *baby rooms* in order to mind the defenceless little children at night.

The budget of the orphanage amounts to $35,000 a year and the supplementary expenses can reach $5,000 a year. The provincial government has contributed a sum of $4,339.32, totalling $0.24 daily per child up to fourteen years of age. The Federation thus provides the entire sum of $30,000 a year for the institution. It is, however, significant that the average maintenance of a child costs $1.30 daily, and food alone costs $0.37.

We could acknowledge that everything was impressive and beautiful: nice rooms; bright, sunny verandas; a fine radio; gramophone; a splendidly beautiful neighbourhood; and "what else do you want, my dear?" But this beautiful *rose*, the Westmount orphanage, unfortunately has one small flaw that exceeds almost all of its merits!

Read on.

What do we expect of a Jewish orphanage? To raise Jewish children according to the Jewish spirit, to bequeath to them, to some degree, the tradition that they would have received from their parents, to plant in them a *Jewish kernel* so that in the future they do not move away from, but rather grow closer to, the Jewish People. In short, the orphanage must provide these children, who have been punished by fate, with a pure Jewish education and endow them with a national pride that will serve as a substitute for a mother or father in life's difficult hours ...

But we will not dwell any further on this type of education. Everyone knows, it would seem, that the orphans in Westmount are altogether *living wanderers*. Still, we maintain that it would never have occurred to anyone that the Westmount School Board would not agree that the orphanage children be permitted to study together with their own children in the Westmount schools! To whom would it have occurred that Westmount would blockade itself behind a Great Wall of China against the Jews from downtown and would force the orphans to be sent to a school all the way on Berthelet Street, where the trip alone back and forth takes two hours every day ...?

Let us put aside for a moment the *pedantries* that the travel actually costs $1,200 a year: At lunchtime, the children are brought to the Baron de Hirsch Institute, where they get their dinner, because this is much closer than bringing them to Westmount. Then they are brought from the Baron de Hirsch Institute back to school, and at around four o'clock, the exhausted and anxious children return to their nest in the orphanage. Only then do they return to their studies in Hebrew! Although this is one of our chief tenets, the fact is that the children, living in this foreign environment, are apathetic to it. The teachers who have to *plant yidishkayt* in these circumstances are not to be envied ...

For this reason, the teaching of Hebrew is a very distressing problem, despite the fact that in the past year [Y. Fuks] as head, Mrs. [Konovitch], and Miss [Levitt] have made great efforts in this area. One senses that the children are beginning to feel something, to grasp something about Jewish history and the wandering Jewish way of life. A spark of sentiment for Zion and Hebrew is awakening in their young hearts, but this is still very far from the goal.

Is this a trifle? To rouse children in the worst frosts of winter no later than six o'clock and rush them through breakfast, getting dressed, and so on so that they are able to arrive at school on time?! In this particular case and under these conditions, this is truly a necessity. This is, however, a heartless way to treat small, defenceless children who have been cursed in their earliest youth.

It works out like this: travel from the orphanage to school, from school to dinner, from dinner back to school, and then from school home ... And only then may they take up the study of the Hebrew language.

What a strain it is to ensure that all of the children were at dinner these days. This [is the] task of the women's committee, which helps out at dinner at Federation ... Escorting *all of the boys* through all of the streetcars and watching that nothing, G-d forbid, should befall anyone is like a daily *small moving army* that manoeuvres without end. And being in transit is many times more costly than keeping them in one place. And all of this is due to what? Because the great authorities in Westmount do not want the local Jewish children to congregate with their children in the same school! And, incidentally, as orphans, no one pays school taxes for them, and poor Westmount cannot provide these few dozen poor orphans with schooling ...

Do things need to be this way in this day and age? Don't poor, forlorn orphans often grow up to be greater personalities than the children of richer parents? Why should this unjust separation exist between one child and another? What are they guilty of?

It is clear that this is an unhealthy development and that the primary task of a Jewish orphanage is to raise healthy and proud Jewish children. However, we do not understand how this is possible under these exceptional circumstances.

Anti-Semitism

In the early decades of the twentieth century, anti-Semitism was flowering. The following adds another dimension to this issue. At Aberdeen School on Saint-Denis Street, a teacher's anti-Semitism spurred a scholars' strike. John Kalbfleisch writes that "this article is adapted from one of his weekly columns on Montreal's history which appeared in the *Gazette*, Sunday, March 3, 2002, page A16, Section: Editorial/Op-Ed."

Anti-Semitism at Aberdeen School

"I am using all my influence to close the matter of the strike at Aberdeen School, and I think it is safe to say that all the Jewish scholars will be at their desks on Monday morning," said Rabbi Abramowitz, when discussing the recent scholars'

> strike as a result of some remarks alleged to have been made by one of the teachers and acted hastily upon by a number of the Jewish scholars attending that institution.
>
> *Gazette*, Saturday, March 1, 1913

It was, according to Reuben Brainin, "the latest sensation." He was writing in the *Keneder Adler*, the influential Yiddish-language newspaper he edited in Montreal, and there is no doubting his dissatisfaction with the offensive remarks the teacher made. Nor is there any doubting the pride he felt in the response of the children. "A major contribution to Jewish renaissance," he would call it.

"A teacher insulted the pride of the Jews," Brainin wrote. "The Jewish students of Aberdeen School on Saint-Denis Street went on strike because, according to their explanations, a teacher of grade six, Miss McKinley, had insulted the feelings of the Jewish students by saying that Jews are dirty."

Jewish immigration to Montreal had increased greatly in the decade or so before World War I. By 1913, there were at least five hundred Jewish students at Aberdeen School, and they had begun to outnumber the gentiles there.

"For some disgruntled Protestants," Israel Medres wrote in his charming memoir, *Montreal of Yesterday*, "this state of affairs was intolerable."

The hapless Miss McKinley apparently complained that, while the school had once been quite clean, it had become far less so with the Jewish influx. She said she would propose to the school committee that henceforth Jews be excluded. This was all a bit much for five students in particular, Joe Orenstein, Moses Margolis, Frank Sherman, Harry Singer, and Moses Skibelsky, who would have been eleven or twelve years old. They decided to go on strike unless the teacher apologized, and when—surprise, surprise—no apology was forthcoming, they were determined to show they weren't bluffing. But when they arrived at the school that Friday morning to pick up their things, they found McKinley had locked the doors. Undaunted, the boys managed to dispatch younger students from class to class to urge everyone to join in and—surprise, surprise, at least surely to McKinley—most of Aberdeen's Jewish students did.

They streamed out of the school, across Saint-Denis Street, and into Carré Saint-Louis. There, emulating strikers among their elders, they appointed a strike committee to act in their behalf. They resolved there would be no breaking of ranks; anyone who abandoned the strike and returned to class would be branded a scab. They delegated some of their number to picket the school and finally—and quite audaciously—they demanded McKinley be fired.

Leaders of the Jewish community were quick to respond. Clearly, they sympathized with the students, but they also were anxious to see the incident wrapped up as quickly as possible. Rabbi Herman Abramowitz of Sha'ar Hashomayim Synagogue and S. W. Jacobs, a prominent lawyer who was president of the Baron de Hirsch Institute, agreed to intervene. They met with Aberdeen's principal, a man named Caulfield, and the children's teacher was at last induced to apologize (although, like so many people caught speaking out of turn, she claimed she had been misunderstood). It was also agreed all the striking students would be readmitted to class without penalty.

Astonishingly, Abramowitz and Jacobs even won the promise that a transfer of the teacher to another position would be considered. The *Gazette*, while all this was going on, was not amused.

This short editorial that appeared Saturday deserves to be quoted in full:

> A big foot should be put down on any strike movement among scholars in public schools. Children are sent to school to be taught by teachers and not to dictate to them, as some of the learned youngsters think in these days of the idle strap and ruler. Let the juveniles wait 'til they grow up to be big men of eighteen and twenty before they begin agitating and worrying old people of thirty and forty. Alas, not a word about what provoked the agitating and worrying in the first place.

> Reubin Brainin's reaction was more nuanced. While glossing over the rights or wrongs of the original remarks and the subsequent strike, he told readers of the *Keneder Adler* the protesters really should have been the students' parents.
>
> "But what interests me," he continued, "is that the children did not seek justice for themselves. It was their national sensibility that was offended and that provoked their little fists against their highest government (for to children, their teachers and schools are the highest government).
>
> "We need to think much about this first sprouting of a generation which is new in our exile history, a free generation which is discarding the chains of Diaspora, which no longer bends its head, no longer begs for justice, but takes what is not accorded it freely."

As we all know, anti-Semitism is still alive and well in the Montreal of today.

The Montreal Home

A big attraction for the children is in the summer when they spend two months in the country in Shawbridge, where the orphanage has its own farm—truly an extraordinary plus. Following is the translation of *Keneder Adler*'s 1931 version.

> *The Orphanage in Westmount*, M. Ginzburg
> Number 12 of the series *Jewish Institutions in Montreal*
> August 10, 1931
>
> ***The Summer Residence in Shawbridge***
> The children of the Jewish orphanage spend the summer months in their own well-equipped summer residence in Shawbridge. Although this residence is in use ten to twelve weeks of the year and is locked the other forty, it has become an institution that occupies a very significant position and has quite a bit of history behind it.
>
> The summer residence in Shawbridge, as recuperation and recreation for forlorn Jewish orphans, has already been in exis-

tence for over two decades. Like all other institutions that came into being at that time, it was born through the initiative of a group of Jewish women who had set for themselves a goal of providing poor Jewish children, and above all Jewish orphans, with fresh air and good supervision during the summer months. And just like all Jewish institutions of that time, the summer residence was maintained by the dues of its members and naturally did not have a strong [financial] foundation. The *summer residence* would carry on with difficulty summer after summer, creating new deficits and seeking to cover them later during the winter.

Naturally, this situation could not continue for long, especially with the number of children growing from year to year. In 1914, the heads of the orphanage came to the women's committee of the summer residence with a practical proposal: They would take in the poor children and orphans from the orphanage under the condition that they be *equal partners* of the summer residence in Shawbridge, that is, that the children from the orphanage be able to enjoy the children's camp during the summer months to the same extent as their own children. After some negotiation, an understanding was reached. In that same year, the heads of the orphanage, in practice, operated the summer residence in Shawbridge. These combined strengths greatly facilitated the struggle for existence of the summer residence.

The president of the orphanage at that time, Mr. Vineberg, in particular, put much effort [into the project] during the three years of his leadership from 1913 to 1916. In 1917, when the newly created Federation also took over the management of the orphanage, many improvements were introduced. The summer residence *blossomed* and the number of children reached around fifty. The building consisted of two wings with the children housed in one wing and the staff in another. This is how things remained for five whole years.

The heads at that time unfortunately made one big error. The summer residence in Shawbridge was located in a dry wooden building, vulnerable to fire at the slightest spark. And so it was there, in this nest of orphans, that a great tragedy struck that has had no equal in the history of Jewish Montreal. During the night of August 16–17, 1922, when the children were just about to leave the orphanage and return to the city for the beginning of the school year, a fire broke out which was caused by an overturned kerosene lamp, and in fifteen minutes, the entire farm of the orphanage and eight innocent orphans were burned to coals! The supervisor and his three children also lost their lives in the flames.

If not for the extraordinary efforts of the two orphan brothers, the fourteen- and fifteen-year-old Sammy and [J. Kaufman], if not for the help of the young boys from the nearby training school and the volunteer firemen, who knows how many little orphans would, G-d forbid, have paid with their lives! There were, after all, fifty-three children. The fire came at dawn when the children were submerged in their deep sleep and the flaming tongues swallowed everything around them! ...

There were, at that time, no fire escapes and the children had to be rescued from the second floor with ladders made out of torn sheets and blankets.

It cannot be imagined how great and terrible the tragedy was. Many children were paralyzed by fear; others remained with *frights* on their faces for their entire lives. Montreal Jewry was unable to console them for months after the terrible catastrophe.

At first, anger and wrath were expressed at the funeral committee who had arranged it so that not a single Orthodox rabbi eulogized the orphans, and even worse, the children's bones were held overnight in a Christian undertaker's and brought over in a Christian hearse. This greatly touched the religious–national sentiments of all of the Jews present and the remorse was very strong. Everyone complained: "If it was not possible to have a purely Orthodox funeral in Westmount, the children should have been brought to a Jewish neighbourhood..."

* * *

A picture—recently taken by Harry Pinker—of the monument honouring the children appears in the first photo section. All the children's names and ages at their death are engraved on a stone plaque.

Perpetual care for the plot is paid for by the Baron de Hirsch Institute. "To view it is very moving," says Roslyn Raginsky Liverant, who arranged to have this photo taken, and whose family was very involved in the Montefiore Home from the 20s to the early 40s.

* * *

And this is another confirmation of what we have already said in our previous article about the orphanage in Westmount: that the Jewish soul and the Jewish spirit are missing. At the head of a Jewish orphanage must stand people for whom yidishkayt is not an incidental or excess burden, but a concern that is truly serious. These orphans are not the children of this or that president or from this or that part of town; these are children of Jewish Montreal and all Montreal Jews are mothers to them. This is how the orphan problem has always been addressed and must continue to be addressed in the future.

The complaints, however, brought results. The heads of the social organizations realized that holding a position also means great duties and responsibilities.

In 1924, a new summer building in Shawbridge was erected but not [*sic*] with much more care than the earlier one. And, at present, the camp consists of about thirty acres of land. The house has no upper floors. The children are always located downstairs on both sides of the building. There are many exits in case of emergency. The electricity has been set up with protective devices so that no fire takes place.

The summer residence is located in a splendidly beautiful area ... all sorts of features ... make it comfortable and pleasant for the children. Right by the house runs a beautiful, shallow river where the older children bathe freely. For the younger children, a fenced-in area has been constructed ... Directly on the other side of the river begin the wonderful Laurentian Mountains which bewitch the eye with their unique terraces and landscapes and at which one can never tire of gazing. Dotting the landscape lie individual houses belonging to farmers and city dwellers who have also thought to take advantage of this beautiful corner for their summer vacations ...

And here, in the lap of nature, the Westmount orphans spend two to three summer months after a full year of wandering and strain.

Although, even here, the children are not entirely free. They do daily gymnastic activities under the supervision of an instructor. They study Hebrew leisurely so that they do not forget the bit that they have gained during the winter. The children who are already working independently come out to the summer residence almost every weekend to take in the fresh air and renew their vigour to continue their work.

Here the orphan-children family fully enjoys the rays of the sun, and satiates itself with the splendour of the summer nature that is so pleasing to everyone, especially to the child and the orphan.

* * *

It is understandable that the summer residence is an invaluable treasure for the children of the Westmount orphanage and could serve a much greater contingent of children than those of the institution.

There is so much more room and so many radiant possibilities to create something grandiose and valuable.

One could not imagine a reason other than the financial difficulties of the Federation that something more significant has not been undertaken.

But the place itself calls: Come, doers, and create new summer nests for the large number of Jewish children who lack fresh air and good nourishment and supervision, at least during the two to three summer months. We shall return to the problem of orphanages after we have visited the Montefiore Orphanage and its summer camp in Sainte-Agathe.

* * *

What did surface, though, was this anecdote of what happened to the home after it closed in 1942. Montrealer Alvin J. Guttman recently wrote the following:

> My wife, Naomi, and I had the pleasure of meeting you both [the Gordons] at the reunion meeting held last year at the Cummings Jewish Centre for Seniors. Although I am not a *graduate* of the MHOH Centres in Montreal, my interest in attending the meeting was due to the fact that I was a resident at the former home located at 500 Claremont from 1944 to October 1945.
>
> In 1942, after having been discharged from military hospital, I was sent to aid in the organization of a Canadian Army Trades Training School. This unit was named the No. 4 Vocational Training School (VTS) and was originally located at the Motordrome Barracks, 312 Sherbrooke Street East, in Montreal.
>
> I was placed in charge of the administration with a staff of eleven military personnel and ten civil servants. Various courses in trades, which the Army required, were conducted for 1,500 soldiers at a time, eight weeks for each course.
>
> In 1944 the No. 4 VTS vacated these barracks and was transferred to 500 Claremont Avenue in Westmount. I probably occupied the very same office that was used by Mr. Max Matt (or the Byes). The unit was disbanded in October 1945, at which time I was discharged to return to civilian life.
>
> I purchased Judy's book, which was enjoyed by both my wife and me. It brought back some memories of some of the people I met, in particular I believe, playing baseball in the old Atwater Baseball League, and if my memory is correct, Sam Rasminsky was on the same team.

Sam was originally in the Montefiore Home, and when it closed in 1936, he was sent to the Montreal Home on Claremont. Myer Gordon recently remembered that Alvin's second cousin, Leo Guttman, who lived on Jeanne-Mance, went to Bancroft School with him and many of the Montefiore Home kids, and Leo used to go with his father to the shul in the home.

Montreal Hebrew Orphans' Home Alumni

(Left) Annie Rosenbaum (rear centre) with her younger brothers Sydney (front centre) and Hyman (front right), their parents and baby Sylvia-prior to 1921 when the three oldest children were admitted to the Montreal Home

Sarah Palmer with son Aaron, still in his Sergeant's uniform from the Fourth Armoured Division

(Below top row) second from right) Annie entered the home on Claremont in 1921. Her two brothers joined her soon after. When she left the home, she changed her name to Gert Rose

(Above) The Berman family: Charles, sister Ann, and brother Sam with their mother (1926)

(Below) Charles Berman with Jack Zukerman and Rose at the 2001 reunion, just two months before his death

August 1, 1993-another MHOH reunion. (Back row) Abe Bye, Harvey Israel, Manny Cohen; (Front row) Raye Bye, Shirley Israel, Shirley (Israel) Thau, Mary Cohen. (Below left) Nathan 'Piggy' and Manny Cohen, 1940 at Sunshine Camp. (Right) Mary & Manny Cohen's wedding day, over 50 years ago!

Manny and Nathan Cohen, unknown, and spouses Hannah & Mary

Florence and Richard Kramer, Sarasota, Florida, meet Myer Gordon to discuss the Westmount Home. (circa 1995) Richard's mother was cook in the 1930s, and it was he who gave us some early home history

Irving Layton at the 1990 reunion, and below with one of Max Matt's sons.

Photos by Myer Gordon

(Left) Annie and Reuben Reisler

(Below) Great pals from the Montreal Home meet at the 1989 reunion: Annie Reisler Thomas, Bernard Turowitz, and Muriel Fishman

(Right) Muriel Fishman and Beatrice Hock, a teen-age volunteer in the Westmount Home-so many years ago.

Sunshine Camp, St. Marguerite (Front row) unknown, Aaron Schmoiser, Eli Miller, unknown, unknown, unknown; (Second row) Sammy Freedman, Billy Aaron, Sammy Ticker, Sammy Schwartz, Frankie Baker, Moishe Miller; (Third row) Manny Cohen, Lester Dick, unknown, unknown, Oscar Roth, Sammy Belinco; (Top row) unknown, Dave Ginsberg, unknown, Jack Gross, unknown.

CIE DES TRAMWAYS DE MONTREAL
TRAMWAYS COMPANY
David Ginsberg
Strathearn High
Secretary-Treasurer
No. 34087
David- Ginsberg- 1938

David Ginsberg's Tramway pass from Strathearn High School

More camp kids from the Montreal Home: Moe Letnick (left), Aaron Schmoiser (fourth from left). Manny Cohen (front) with glasses. Others-recognize yourself?

Montreal Home girls at summer camp in Shawbridge (1928) Annie Mitnick, Minnie Kessler, Esther Plotnick, Nettie Shragie, Mary Boxenbaum

Alvin J. Guttman, lived and worked in the former Montreal Home on Claremont Avenue from 1944 to 1945. The home had closed in 1942, and at that time was used as a military vocational school.

Guttman, ever the ball player, circa 1994!

Meyer Stolov, Montreal Home resident, shown on the left, with his twin brother Ben, who was placed in the Julius Richardson Convalescent Hospital in Chateauguay—1934.

Below left, Meyer, a professional violinist photo 2000.

Below right, the Gordons visit Meyer in Ithaca, N.Y. in 2001

One side of the *Calling Card* from 500 Claremont, the former Montreal Hebrew Orphans' Home-how times change!

(Below) The other side of the card (a map of the area)

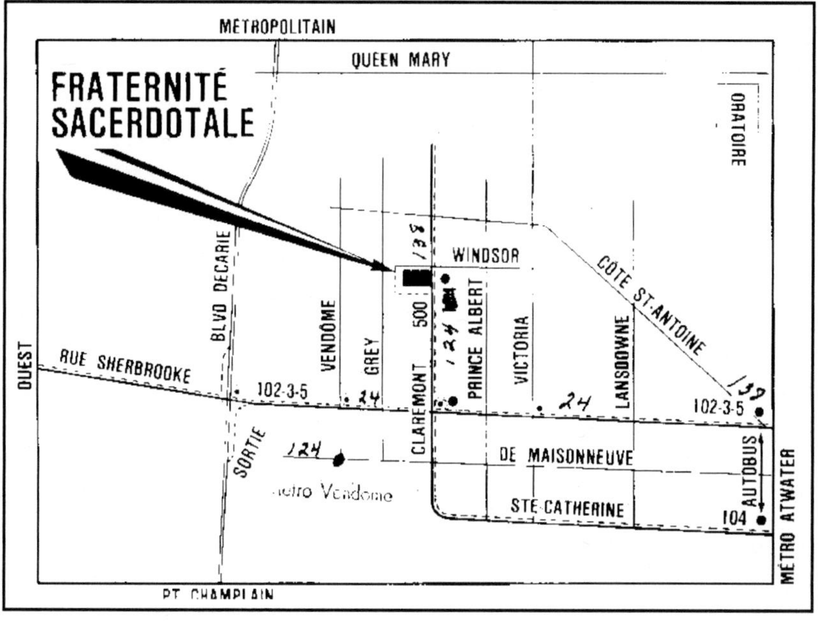

The Montefiore Home

The Montefiore Orphanage, M. Ginzburg
Number 13 of the series *Jewish Institutions in Montreal*
August 18, 1931

One of the most congenial and bright institutions in our city is doubtless the Montefiore Orphanage, which was founded on February 18, 1919, and is located at 4650 Main Street [*sic*].

At that time, the relationship between the downtown and the uptown Jews was very cold and divided. The Jews from downtown, who were mainly immigrants, brought with them from the other side of the ocean warm, sentimental feelings which did not complement the coldly traditional and rigid viewpoint of uptown. Because of this, a group of social activists consisting primarily of women had the idea of establishing an independent Jewish orphanage despite the fact that the Federation already operated its own orphanage on a significant scale.

It should be noted here that thanks to the extensive efforts of Mrs. W. Lustgarten, an initial meeting took place in her house to which she invited Mrs. [Feyge] Steinberg, [J. Ritz], [Fishkin], [Rubin], [Zilberberg], [Kivenko], Friedman, [Henkin], [Chaiman], [Berman], [Bloomfield], [Zudik], Diamond, Gibson, [Cooperman], Goodman, Miller [who, with her husband, Julius B., was among the founders of the home], and [Y. Darabaner]. This was the first official gathering where a press committee was elected [consisting] of Mrs. [Ascher] Cooper, Mrs. Abramowitz (present chair of the Admission Committee), [A.] Berman as secretary, Mr. H. [Hirsch] Hershman, and Mrs. M. Rosenstein.

Initially, these meetings were taken up by purely organizational questions. By March 24, 1919, it was decided to find a home in order to faster transform the idea into a reality. Because the provisional committee consisted of too many members and it was difficult to gather everyone in private homes, on May 12, an executive was elected with Mr. M. Abramowitz as president, Ascher Cooper as treasurer and H. Hershman as secretary. They worked very intensively until September 29, when official elections of all [Home] members took place. At that time, Mr. M.

Abramowitz was elected president, Mrs. W. Lustgarten and Mrs. [Zudik] as vice-presidents, Mrs. Rosenstein as recording secretary, Mr. Cooper as treasurer, Mr. H. Hershman and Mr. [Trihub] as comptroller, and Mrs. [Zilberberg], Mrs. [Taube], and Mr. [Spiegel] as trustees.

A board of directors was specially chosen made up of the following individuals: Mrs. Lustgarten, Mrs. Goodman, Mrs. Berman, Mrs. Cohen, Mrs. Diamond, Mrs. [Fishkin], Mrs. [Bloomfield], Mr. Gibson and Mrs. C. B. Feiner. The elected house committee consisted of M. Abramowitz as president and Philip [Weinstein].

The meetings were moved to Prince Arthur Hall. There were difficulties in purchasing a house and this delayed the speedy realization of the plan. For this reason, at the meeting of December 8, a committee was elected for the purpose of negotiating with the Federation in order to seek a means of settlement.

The negotiations, however, did not meet with success, and, after a long and arduous search, a church on Main Street [*sic*] was purchased from the *Subotgires* [Russian Christian sect of Sabbath observers]. A sum of $10,000 was allotted to renovate the house and to render it suitable [for use] as an orphanage.

We digress...

The following valuable information came to the fore immediately after the original *Four Hundred Brothers and Sisters* was published. Its writer, architect Sue Bronson, lives directly across the street from the Jeanne-Mance site of the Montefiore Home. She did research for her final PhD dissertation on the history of the former *Mile-End Exhibition Grounds*, within which the home was located. Her notes provide some background.

> The building that used to house the Montefiore Hebrew Orphans' Home occupies a double lot on Jeanne-Mance Street, about halfway between Mount Royal Avenue and Villeneuve Street. It stands out from its neighbours, all of which are two- and three-storey row houses, because it is the only building on the street with a side yard (which later served as a playground for the orphans), and it has a distinctive corner entrance.

It is part of a large property that was occupied, from 1870 until 1898, by the *Mile-End Exhibition Grounds*; the streets, lanes, and lots were traced in 1898, and most of the buildings on the block were constructed between 1905 and 1910. The area was known as the *Village of Saint-Louis du Mile-End* from 1878 until 1895, then as the *Town of Saint-Louis* from 1895 until 1910. On January 1, 1910, the Town of Saint-Louis was annexed and became the *Laurier Ward of the City of Montreal.* Today, the property is part of the Mile-End District of Montreal's *Plateau Mont-Royal Borough.*

The annual assessment rolls for the property reveal that 4650–52 Jeanne-Mance was not yet under construction in May 1909, but ... was underway in May 1910, and complete by 1911 ... The owner at the time of the construction was Jacob C. Cassel, gentleman and clergyman. In 1911, he occupied the second-floor flat, and David Smeal, manager, occupied the third floor; the ground floor was the Mount Royal Brethren Church. In 1916, the Mount Royal Brethren Church still occupied the ground floor (and presumably the basement), and its pastor, Thomas H. Broad, clergyman, occupied the second-floor flat; the third-floor flat was occupied by Joseph H. Golt, merchant. It must have been around 1920 that the building was sold to the orphanage, because the 1920–21 Lovell's Directory still lists the Mount Royal Brethren Church as the occupant of the ground floor; at that time, W. J. Hemphill occupied the middle flat, and the Victorian Order of Nurses occupied the top floor.

* * *

Our original 'info' in Book One noted that the newly created Montefiore Hebrew Orphans' Home was said to have opened in 1918—run by the Jewish community. It seems it was at the discussion stage only. The building was run by Federation after that home closed in 1936—until the 1980s. The Herzl Dispensary occupied the facility at some point following the closure in 1936.

* * *

In 1921, however, the following names were listed on the assessment roll as the owners of the *Orphan Hospital*: Julius Benjamin Miller, Asher Cooper, Max Rosenstein, Marcus Abramowitz,

Hiram Abramovitch, and Sam Spigler. [It is possible that the spelling of some of these names is incorrect.]

The assessment rolls also reveal the changes in the assessed values of the land (a double lot) and the building. The part(s) of the building that served as a place of worship, and then as an orphanage, was (were) exempt from municipal taxes. The changes in property assessments over time were consistent with those of most of the other lots and buildings on the street.

	Land	Building	Total	Tax exemption
1911	3,400	10,600	14,000	4,000
1916	7,100	11,900	19,000	12,700
1921	6,550	19,950	26,500	26,500

Notes on the Charter (Lois et Statuts du Québec, 13 Geo. V, Chapter 122, sanctioned December 29, 1922):

The charter that officially established the Montefiore Hebrew Orphans' Home of Montreal as a corporation was sanctioned on December 29, 1922, at least a year after the orphanage occupied the property on Jeanne-Mance Street.

The following members of Montreal's Jewish community were involved in founding the home, intended to serve the needs of Jewish children whose parents had died or could no longer care for them: Julius Benjamin Miller (merchant), Asher Cooper (merchant), Moses Feldman (merchant), Robert Gradinger (merchant), Nathan Blau (fur manufacturer), Hiram Abramovitch (merchant), Marcus Abramowitz, Max Rosenstein, Charles Schachter (merchant), Berush Steinhouse (furniture merchant), Max Seigler (insurance broker), David Sperber (gentleman), Saul Lerner (auditor), Feivel Seidman (novelties merchant), Benny Udashkin (butcher), Sam Spigler, Max Handman (tailor), Max Wall (accountant), Harry Schnaiberg (manufacturer).

This provincial law stated that the property owned by members of the corporation (listed above) was transferred to the corporation; presumably the property in question was 4650–52 Jeanne-Mance Street. It gave the corporation the power to acquire other property, to carry out property transactions, to receive donations and inheritances, etc.

It was to establish its own bylaws, in accordance with provincial law, to hire staff, and to operate the orphanage. It stated that none of the members of the corporation could be held personally responsible for the debts of the corporation. The corporation was required to provide information on its assets to the provincial government upon request.

Susan Bronson
August 27, 2002

More from Sue later ...

In 1921 the house was completed and could accommodate sixty-four beds. The number of children at the beginning was very small, but with time, more children joined them and the institution took its rightful position in the philanthropic and social life of Montreal.

The name, Montefiore Home, was the suggestion of Mr. Harry Hershman who had gone to great efforts on behalf of the new institution. Speaking of the name *Montefiore*, let me digress for a moment and hopefully give you a chuckle.

Isn't the Internet wonderful? Or not! On the one hand, the brief but dignified and informative bio of Moses Montefiore, included in the original *Four Hundred Brothers and Sisters*, came from there, as did this joke, which landed on my desktop. I couldn't resist using it here:

> Moses Montefiore, the great nineteenth-century philanthropist, once found himself seated next to an anti-Semite nobleman at a dinner party. "I have just returned from Japan," the nobleman was saying, "and it is a most unusual country. Did you know that it has neither pigs nor Jews?" "In that case," Montefiore replied, "you and I should go there, so it will have a sample of each."

Back to the translation ...

The fee for members was $3 per year. It must, however, be emphasized that not one of the other Jewish institutions evoked as much popularity and love among Montreal Jewry as the Montefiore Orphanage. It should also be acknowledged that this was not for nothing. The love and devotion that the downtown Jews displayed toward the home and the lively spirit that was breathed into the institution continues to beat with a strong pulse to this day.

Wonder upon wonder, the Montefiore Orphanage is the only institution that maintains itself independently through voluntary charitable contributions. Although the weekly budget ranges from $550 to $600 a week and there are no special funds, the organization meets its expenses in an exemplary manner and has no deficit to the present day.

This indicates that the battle for survival is fought day in, day out, tirelessly and successfully.

There have been three stages of development for the Montefiore Orphanage in the ten years of its existence.

The first stage, ending in 1925 was, if one can use the term, the *romantic* stage. Montreal Jews expressed very strong sympathies when rejoicing in the success of the institution. The second stage took place under the presidency of Mr. M. Feldman. The number of children increased substantially so that it became impossible to accommodate all of them. At the annual meeting, the president recommended the addition of a new building to better be able to meet the needs of the thirty-eight children and nineteen refugees from Europe who were living in the orphanage, a total of fifty-seven children.

The recommendation was adopted and it was decided to begin the building project. This naturally resulted in high costs. Due to the expansions on the home, new children streamed in until the number quickly reached eighty-six.

In May 1927, the Montefiore Orphanage undertook a fund-raising campaign to raise $40,000.

It turned out that daily concerns for the future were weakening the broader activities of the administration. The $40,000 was intended to erase the deficit of $10,000 with $30,000 to serve for the ongoing annual budget. At the head of the campaign was Max Seigler (current president) and the capital campaign was crowned with success. The rattling of the collection box was able to stop for the moment.

It should also be mentioned that Mr. Lyon Cohen, Rabbi Dr. Abramowitz, President Feldman, Mr. H. Wolofsky, Mr. Clarence Michaels, [Berl] Schwartz (current alderman), Mr. [Isaac] Silverstone, and Mr. [Steinman] held brilliant lectures at the campaign meeting.

This period could be characterized as highly successful if not for the regrettable scandal which resulted from the mismanagement of funds by the former administrator in which the young institution lost almost $5,000.

The general meeting which took place at the end of 1928 implemented the following changes in the makeup of the officers, namely: S. W. Jacobs and Mr. M. Feldman as honorary presidents, B. Gradinger as honorary vice-president, Mr. L. B. Daniels as president, Mr. A. Raginsky, Mr. [Y. M. Rubinovitch] and L. [Daitsher] as vice-presidents, Mr. M. [Shneiderman] as treasurer, Mr. S. Lerner as financial secretary, Mrs. D. Cohen as secretary and the ladies [*sic*] [Lustgarten, Gibson and [Ross] as honorary members. This *cabinet* remained in place for two years and it can be labelled the third period up to the present in the activity of the Montefiore Orphanage.

During the course of two years, much was accomplished. The repercussions of the financial losses had a very negative effect on the spirits of the home's friends and sympathizers. The Board of Directors was involved in keeping the orphanage afloat financially and got people from the Jewish community involved. Mr. Raginsky put great efforts into clarifying that no one was actually to blame for the financial losses. He awakened affection and sympathy among the members with his calls for further support of this important institution.

* * *

Two generations of Raginskys were involved at the Montefiore Home, beginning in 1918 when it opened—it became a family project as they became involved in all aspects of the facility! Granddaughter Roslyn Raginsky Liverant sent in some family history and photos.

Abraham Raginsky joined the Board in 1924 and served as president in the 30s; his wife, Anna Sr., was also a director and on the

Ways and Means Committee. Their son, Alexander O. Raginsky, and his wife, Gertrude Illievitz, served on several committees and outings for the orphans and the camp. We lived just five blocks away from the Claremont orphanage, so it was very easy, my sister says, for my dad to walk to that home. Although ... the family efforts were mainly directed toward Jeanne-Mance 'til it closed.

Dr. A. B. Illievitz, Gertrude's brother—who received his medical degree in 1918—was the home's medical director from the earliest years, surgeon-in-chief at Herzl Hospital and Dispensary, and a Baron de Hirsch medical director from 1933 to 1945; Abraham Raginsky was also a director, 1924–42.

Employment was given to several female orphans upon leaving the orphanage at the family's bedding and furniture company, Dominion Bedding. As well, beds and furniture were donated to the orphanages in the 1930s.

Later on, I think some of the orphans also went to Camp B'nai Brith, with which my father was involved, and also—in later years—received help from the Hebrew Free Loan Organization.

My mother, Gert, went to (the infamous) Aberdeen School, as did my sister who took her training there for the Montreal Oral School for the Deaf.

Both Abraham and Alexander O. Raginsky died in 1942 (ten weeks apart) as the remaining orphanage closed its door—their good deeds done! What a wonderful legacy my grandfather and father left their children.

* * *

The new president, Mr. L. B. Daniels, likewise did not want to dwell on the past and sought the means by which the orphanage could be dragged out of its negative state. During the course of the first year, the result was so great that not only was the earlier deficit covered but a surplus of \$7,665 remained, despite the fact that the budget amounted to \$27,015.

This resulted in much enthusiasm and passion among the officers and they threw themselves into a new year of work.

Another banquet was held for the purpose of covering the mortgage of \$17,000 in order to free the institution from this oppressive debt. Mr. Raginsky was the first to pledge $200, and his example inspired others to follow. Alderman Seigler introduced a project to create a bronze plaque for the first 175 names to contribute a minimum of $100. The banquet raised $5,300 on the spot, including a contribution of $500 from Mrs. [J. Finestone] in memory of her deceased husband [J. Finestone], former chairman of the Vaad Ha'ir [Jewish Community Council].

In 1929, a successful raffle for $1,000 in gold was held. It is interesting to note that it was [won] by A. Cooper. The winning number was selected by Mayor Houde (at that time, Houde did not yet deem it necessary to capitalize on anti-Semitism). Mr. Cooper, however, exhibited an exemplary example of nobility. He returned $500 to the institution and promised the remaining $500 in writing in annual instalments of $100 over 5 years.

The raffle was very successful and all of the members were very satisfied.

In 1930, Mr. L. B. Daniels resigned as president and Alderman Max Seigler was elected together with almost the same composition of officers as today. During the course of the year, President Seigler managed to obtain the sum of $5,000 from the government that had long been outstanding. There were, however, difficulties in acquiring the funds.

* * *

Edward Daniels wrote to us, one day out of the blue, to say that he still has the kiddish cup given to his grandfather by the children in the home, a memento of his many kindnesses to them. The inscribed cup was presented on May 25, 1933 (see photo).

My grandfather was one of the original founders of the Montefiore Hebrew Orphans' Home and then became president. At the same time, he was also a president of the Montreal Hebrew Old Peoples' Home.

I remember that he personally selected Dr. Harry Sinclair right out of medical school to be the doctor for the home. He opened an office next door and became so well known that he was asked to be the physician for the old folks' home. He also later became the family doctor for the Daniels family.

> Unfortunately, my grandfather passed away three years after the 1933 presentation, and the orphans in the home followed the hearse right to the cemetery ... I, too, followed in his footsteps when I became president, in 1987, of the Young Men's–Young Women's Hebrew Association of Montreal.

The achievements of people like Mr. Daniels ensured that the homes were well maintained and the children received the best of care under the sometimes very trying conditions.

* * *

Marilyn Gomberg Silver, of the Toronto area, wrote that her father's grandmother, Rose Ram, used to fundraise, by going door-to-door, for the Montefiore Home in the late 1920s and 30s. Her father also recalls that a painting she had done hung at the entrance to the home.

More Yiddish translation ...

The next article will discuss the educational side of the Montefiore Orphanage and the summer camp in Sainte-Agathe as well as speak generally about the inner nature of the institution vis-à-vis the Jewish orphan.

> The activity [of the home] is carried out on a wide range and is resulting in commendable achievements. As a result, the Montefiore Home has become a sort of headquarters for all social institutions and is eliciting greater and greater sympathies among Montreal Jews.
>
> *The Montefiore Orphanage*, M. Ginzburg
> Number 14 of the series *Jewish Institutions in Montreal*
> August 25, 1931
>
> "Everything depends on luck, even the Torah in the ark," says an old and very accurate Jewish saying, and it can also be fully applied in relation to the Montefiore Orphanage. The institution was born at a fortunate time and has simply become *the darling* of Montreal Jews.
>
> When you enter the institution, you see how forlorn Jewish orphans have found a home, a bright and tidy home, where dozens of men and women who have been at this holy work for

over ten years do whatever possible to provide the Jewish orphan with a [substitute for a] mother or a father.

The Montefiore Orphanage has children from barely three years of age to sixteen and seventeen years of age. The institution takes in very small, unripe *creations* and lets them out into the world as people when they are more or less ready to choose a field or a trade for which the orphanage has been preparing them during the previous two or three years.

When leaving the institution, the children ... take with them the education that they received in public school with some also having completed two to three years of high school. Secondly, they take with them a wide range of Yiddish and Hebrew knowledge, and third, physical and spiritual life preparation. Simply put, [they leave with a] vocation.

Let us now see to what factors this education owes its existence, to what extent the children actually receive their knowledge from their schools or from the home itself in the area of Yiddish and Hebrew studies and so on. As far as concerns the education and instruction of the children in the schools, it is enough to observe that most of [the orphans] distinguish themselves at graduation and some even receive scholarships in order to further pursue their studies.

This is enough of an indication that the children are not only by no means behind other children, G-d forbid, but that they also belong to the top of the class in their diligence and abilities.

As far as Hebrew and Yiddish studies are concerned, it must be observed that the Montefiore Orphanage gives the children a substantial Jewish and traditional education. It plants in the hearts of the children all of the Jewish virtues and acquaints them with all the customs and traditions that have their source in Jewish life from times immemorial to the present day.

Beginning with the regular prayers, the boys and girls take an equal part, forming a mixed choir which brings amazement to every visitor. It is simply a spiritual delight to observe how older girls and boys sing the authentic Jewish melodies and prayers together which breathe with the loftiness of the ancient Jewish martyred nation. Some kind of a special grace has been granted the Jewish orphans who are incorporated into this Jewish family. They are raised according to the Jewish spirit and swell the ranks of proper Jewish children who are unfortunately becoming fewer and fewer in number here in America.

Jewish studies are divided into four sections and four separate groups to study Yiddish and Hebrew according to the age and abilities of each child. They start with the *alef-beys* and [proceed to] the Chumash [Five Books of Moses], the Na Kh [Prophets and Writings], history, literature, Aggadah [legends] and Midrashim [Homiletic literature], and so on.

The chairman of the educational committee is the well-known, tireless worker, Mr. [Scholem] Lerner, who is simply a fanatic and more loyal to the orphanage than a father to his children. Mr. Lerner follows the Jewish calendar and does not neglect a single important Jewish date where some sort of celebration could be arranged, thereby making the issue at hand clear to the children. For example, every year annual Seders are carried out which make a deep and unforgettable impression on the children. All of the home's close activists are invited and its president addresses the children and warms them with a heartfelt Yiddish word.

The Seder ceremonies are carried out with all of the details in place, to the point that even the *stealing* of the afikomen is practised and every industrious *detective* who finds it receives a prize. The various holidays are marked in true Jewish tradition: Tu Bishvat, Purim, Lag Ba'omer, Hannuka with the lighting of the candles, in addition to the regular traditions of the Sabbaths and holidays, which are meticulously observed according to the rules of Jewish national life. Today, the bar mitzvah celebrations have become a special *institution* in the Montefiore Orphanage. Every bar mitzvah is celebrated with much festivity. The children feel a special pride and the moment truly creates a *monumental day* in their lives.

This indicates that the educational committee is fulfilling its duties at an appropriately high level together with the devoted teacher, Mrs. Shamovitch, who really gives of her entire consciousness and soul to the children. They are planting deeply sentimental, national, religious, and ethical feelings in the children's hearts and are educating the children as proud Jews and, at the same time, as conscious productive citizens of the land.

And if we understand that an orphanage must follow this path, if we can't demand of every father or mother to give their children a national-Jewish education due to different circumstances, we can demand it of a Jewish orphans' institution, sustained thanks to Jewish sympathies and the thousands of Jews who regard themselves as *partners* in this great societal project.

When we speak of the sympathy of Montreal Jews to the Montefiore Orphanage, we must illustrate it with facts.

First of all, Montreal: The Jewish wholesale butchers, thanks to the intervention of the former president of the Vaad Ha'ir, Mr. [Y. Merson], have decided to continually provide the orphanage with free meat of the best quality. This represents a major portion of the budget of the home. The Jewish Barbers' Union of Montreal has had a tradition for years of attending to the children of orphanage entirely free of charge according to the tastes of each child (the barbers also work voluntarily for the Westmount orphanage).

The well-known *Deskin Brothers* clean all of the children's things completely free of charge and return them as good as new. If one enters the *clothing room*, one finds ample new clothes and suits, not only for the coming winter but also for the following summer. There is a cupboard of items, groceries, fruit, and all sorts of good things, and everything is free, at no cost.

We also, however, have to take into account the personal: the bills for gas and electricity, the mortgage and interest, and other expenses. Where do the resources come from to pay for them?

There are more than enough resources, not, G-d forbid, because there is gold lying in the streets, but because the source of Jewish sympathy does not dry up, because there is no Jewish celebration where the Montefiore Orphanage is not mentioned. And not only in Montreal, but cheques and cash come from far away. The bounty grows together with the joy of the seventy Jewish orphans.

Today, special Jewish occasions take place in the actual synagogue of the orphanage by upright and noble Montreal Jews. They value this kind of institution and understand how to create sources of joy and happiness for the unhappy orphans who so desperately need kindness and encouragement.

* * *

Though Fanny Steiner Tessler was not in either of the homes, she thought she and her mother were providing just this to one of the orphans, as she described to us in this story.

Dora Goldstein was born in Constantinople, Turkey, in 1922; her parents came to Canada in 1926. She was put into the Montefiore Home at age five and a half. Fanny's mother would bring her to the home every Saturday to visit and play with Dora. At the end of the day, Fanny and her mother went back to their home. At age sixteen, Dora had to leave the orphanage (the rule was that the children had to leave when they turned sixteen—to live with family, friends, or in their own place). Mrs. Steiner asked Dora to come live with them, but she refused. Why? "Because she was mad at me," Fanny said. During all those years of playing with her in the orphanage, she was not asked to go home with them—"She was mad at my mother and me for leaving her there!"

Fanny says she still cries over this incident, knowing now how hurt Dora must have felt. But, at the time, neither she nor her mother ever realized the harm they were doing; they had thought they were doing a good deed.

In later years, Fanny became friendly with another orphanage resident, Manny Cohen, and his wife, Mary. And she even came to the first reunion! Myer bumped into Fanny again recently at a B'nai Brith Lodge meeting.

* * *

Another serious tidbit comes from Herbert Paperman, whose father, Sam, started the undertaking empire many years ago. We went to Herb—after all, we had used his services for some dear family members—to see if we could interest him in our original book, *Four Hundred Brothers and Sisters*.

He bought some for his sons and left us with this—one of his grandfather's wives had a son, Abe Grossman, who was in the Montefiore Home and is remembered even today by many of the alumni. More Jewish geography!

Back to the translation ...

Thus, prominent Jewish families have recently celebrated their own children's bar mitzvahs [at the orphanage], including Mr. and Mrs. [J. Osman], Mr. and Mrs. S. [Botner], Mr. and Mrs. B. [G. Noskin], Mr. and Mrs. Gerald [Trit], Mr. and Mrs. Max [Gerstman], Mr. and Mrs. [A. Y. Miller], the Waxman brothers of their nephew Jack [Shevsky]. Mr. and Mrs. [A. Shneiderman] (treasurer of the Montefiore Orphanage), who joyfully celebrated the bar mitzvah of their son, Isidore, with a fabulous party for all of the children as well as for the nursing home. During the event, the bar mitzvah boy distributed among the children a significant sum of money that he had saved himself.

Mr. and Mrs. [Jay Baker] celebrated the bar mitzvah of their son, Sydney. Mr. [Baker] regularly volunteers his labour and effort as a plumbing contractor for the orphanage and the celebration brought in $150 from the guests. Mr. and Mrs. Voskoff celebrated the birthday of their daughter, Shirley, with a big party for the children of the home and distributed lovely presents to the orphans. Mr. and Mrs. Samuel Friedman (from the *Keneder Adler*) did the baby naming for their daughter in the synagogue of the Montefiore Orphanage. Mr. and Mrs. D. Cohen (recording secretary of the home for the last eight years) celebrated their golden wedding anniversary in the institution. The birthdays of vice-president [Y. M. Rabinovitch] and of the president, Alderman Max Seigler, were celebrated at the Montefiore Orphanage.

When the friends and supporters of Mr. and Mrs. W. Lustgarten celebrated the housewarming for their newly purchased house, the party was led to the [Montefiore] Home and with it, many donations. Mr. and Mrs. David [Zolov] have established a tradition of distributing presents to the orphaned children every Hannuka.

A worker in the [Friedman]'s clothing company got sick and the workers collected $58, but by then the worker had died. What happened to the $58? It went to the Montefiore Orphanage, to poor orphans because this is *the next best thing*. What else does a deceased worker leave behind if not orphans?! ...

Here is another interesting incident involving $6: Mr. B. [Clayman] was (heaven forfend!) sitting shiva and, as a member of Hebrew Sick Benefit Society, he received $6 in the mail as compensation for wages lost sitting shiva. This is the tradition of the Hebrew Sick Benefit Society. [Clayman], however, is a man of sentiment and a Jewish heart. He said that sitting shiva is a mitzvah and has to be done for its own sake. While according to the constitution he had to accept the $6, he forwarded the check to the Montefiore Orphanage ... It is not more than $6 but what noble sentiment lies behind it.

When Mr. Aaron Wolofsky got engaged to be married, the cash register of the orphanage received $30. There are endless cases like this.

It is impossible to list the hundreds and thousands of donors or all the people who link their moral delight with the success of the Montefiore Home. Even at the smaller celebration of a poor Jewish worker, moneys are sent to the Montefiore Orphanage. These small contributions are the finest expression of their relationship with the Jewish institution and are equal to the biggest contributions of the wealthiest Jews.

* * *

Miriam Peletz came to our *read* at Montreal's Temple Emanu-el November 2003. When she came over afterwards to purchase a book, she insisted on paying $28, not the regular $25 cost. She had a most interesting reason. In 1935, her father, S. Klinger, made a $28 donation in support of the Montefiore Home, as noted in *Four Hundred Brothers and Sisters* on page 107. She wanted her support to equal his! We have been meeting the nicest people!

* * *

When one goes to Papineau, one sees the women of the Ladies' Auxiliary doing good work for the benefit of the Montefiore Home. Their representative, Mrs. L. [Sorkin], was invited to be a member of the Board of Directors.

A letter arrived from the Jews of Sydney, Nova Scotia, about the need of the Montefiore Home with a cheque for $100 to the address of the *Keneder Adler*.

Mr. [Mendl Malek] considered [the matter] and made a donation to the synagogue of the home: a Sefer Torah [Torah scroll], an ark for the Torah, many sforim [holy books], bentshers [booklets with the benediction after meals], and other synagogue accoutrements that have placed the synagogue on a firm foundation and, at the same time, created joy for the children.

When Yizkor [memorial prayer] or another synagogue memorial is recited in the synagogue, the obligation is fulfilled at the Montefiore Orphanage.

There is a Lerner family in Quebec who consistently keeps the institution in mind and sends regular contributions.

Mr. and Mrs. [Igor Berliner] sent an orthophonic Victrola [phonograph] with several dozen of the best classical records.

The traditional annual ball is held at the big hall and piazza of the Mount Royal Hotel and the success is always noteworthy. Not long ago, a midnight concert was held in Sainte-Agathe where the children spent the last summer in a splendidly beautiful summer residence. The concert raised over $400.

* * *

Ida Sklar Lewis, a Montefiore alumna, recently recounted some memories of the physical layout of the summer camp: "The land was given to the Jewish community and the Board of the Montefiore Home. There was already an older building on the land—which is where the girls slept. The boys slept in tents on the grounds. The Board oversaw the construction of a tennis court and the addition of a dining room-kitchen overlooking the lake—from which water was pumped up to the building." It was these hoses, these hot hoses, that burned the bottoms of Myer Gordon's feet one summer as he ran across the grass, resulting in a stay in *sick bay*—he can still feel the charred, painful skin.

This summer locale was called simply *The Country*. When the Montefiore closed in 1936, the Claremont home moved its camp to this site, renaming it *Sunshine Camp* (as their other camps had been named).

* * *

> Do you want to know the source of the strength and sympathy of the Montefiore Orphanage? We can tell you: it lies in the popularity of the institution which not only connects with the familiar elements of Jewish observance but also seeks the cooperation of all of the Jewish corporate bodies of Montreal. At every possible opportunity, schools, syndicates, benefit societies, and cultural and social organizations are invited. Each of these has free access to the institution, each one is welcome on the premises, and this creates chains of friends and sympathizers. This is the best union between the people and the home.
>
> Of all of the hundreds and thousands of friends [of the institution], a special circle of women has emerged, aside from those discussed in our previous article, who create a loving and warm atmosphere around the institution. One can regularly find the loving Mrs. Beecher, Rosovitch, Schafer, [Shneiderman], [Lefkort], [Coppershtok], Weissberg, Mrs. L. B. Daniels, A. Cooper, [J. Dubrovsky], [Brody], [Mirsky], [A. Stamner], Mrs. B. [Taube], Mrs. Crelinstein, D. Cohen and many, many others who will have to forgive me if I have not mentioned their names. Ha Rav [Dubinsky], Ha Rav [Berner], the teacher, preacher and [cantor] Mendelson, Mr. [Lazinsky], the principal of the Saint-Urbain Street Talmud Torah, Ha Rav [Vachtfogel] and often also Lawyer [Glazer], Mr. [Belodubovsky], the young Abraham [Issac Rosenberg], son of Rabbi Yudel Rosenberg, and many, many others are the examiners, lecturers, friends, and carriers of ideas of the lovely home.
>
> All of this indicates how much love the Montefiore Orphanage earns from everyone and how highly it is held in esteem by everyone.

* * *

Miriam Young's father was Morris Schneiderman, president of the Montefiore Home for many years, and who used to relate stories about the home. She also came to the Temple talk to finally meet us! She had contacted us some time ago to see if anyone remembered her late father.

She especially recalls him talking about Dr. Gisella Friedman who looked after medical problems there. (Many of us remember Dr. Friedman from the late 1950s, when she was a popular Montreal obstetrician-gynecologist.) When the children were away at camp during the summer, Dr. Friedman would call on Mr. Schneiderman during the night—several times over the season—to drive her up to camp to attend some of the kids who had become ill. In those days it took almost four hours to reach the camp in the Laurentians—there were no highways at that time.

Miriam remembers how dedicated he was to the children. And when it closed, he placed quite a few orphans in good homes, one of whom was Faige Fisher.

Mr. Schneiderman was also active with Talmud Torah, the Jewish General Hospital, the Y, and many others. When he arrived in Canada in 1905, as a young man of fifteen, he was taken in by the Baron de Hirsch Institute, which gave him his start. He was so grateful that he vowed he would give back to the community to the best of his ability.

Miriam's mother, Edith, was also very active in the home with the women's groups. She helped run the bazaars, tag days, and other fund-raising events. She also recalls her father being honoured at one of the Montefiore Home's reunions in 1960; this fourth reunion was held at the Ritz Carlton Hotel.

The Montreal Home held its own reunions over the same period. Both as children and adults, the alumni never knew of the other home—of one another. It wasn't until the late 1980s that the first combined reunion was held in Toronto. (More on the latest reunion soon.)

Back to the translation ...

Over all of this watches the vigilant eye of Mr. Sh. Talpis, superintendent of the institution. He upholds the honour and credit of every member and every single person who contributes something to the home and he does not neglect any of the donors. He always publicizes every [donor's] name and shows the appropriate respect and regard to everyone. This is a special plus for the institution as it expands the circle of friends and supporters and the popularity for the home that has made it a centre of Jewish life in Montreal.

Mrs. Rachel as matron also deserves recognition for her capabilities and experience. Also Mr. Matt, himself a former orphan, understands very well his function as supervisor and instructor. In this way, the whole ensemble is one fine orchestra which functions with pride and dignity, regardless of the small, limited salaries that they receive.

Last week, former nurse, Mrs. Milstein, ceased her work. She had contributed her very devoted work to the orphanage for close to five years, with no distinction between day and night. This is a loss for the children and they will feel it keenly.

So, do we have to have two separate [Jewish] orphanages in Montreal and maintain two separate institutions, separate personnels, and two almost identical budgets? In the current state of Montreal Jewry, [they are] liable for sustaining two institutions. Is this kind of division really necessary? More about all of this, and a real conclusion, in our third article.

(This third article never appeared, according to Eiran Harris.)

Instead, more from Sue Bronson ...

In 1966, the assessment rolls list the owner of the building as the Federation of Jewish Philanthropies of Montreal. By this time, the assessed value had risen to $63,300 ($14,250 for the land and $49,050 for the building); this entire amount was subjected to a municipal tax exemption "for orphanage"; although the building no longer served as an orphanage, it was used for community and healthcare purposes.

In 1986, the assessment rolls list the property owner as the Allied Jewish Community Services of Montreal (at 5151 Côte Sainte-Catherine Road), but it was noted that the building was occupied by the community health clinic, CLSC Saint-Louis du Parc. Its assessed value had increased to $158,400 ($18,000 for the land and $140,400 for the building), which was relatively consistent with the assessed values of the other properties on the street.

It was probably shortly after this that the property was sold. Today, the ground floor and basement are occupied by a daycare, Garderie Villeneuve, and the two upper floors are occupied by L'Hirondelle, Services d'accueil et d'intégration des immigrants (an organization that offers welcome and integration services for immigrants).

Thus, throughout its history, the property has served both the neighbourhood and the community at large, and healthcare, childcare, religion, and immigrants have been consistently recurrent themes in its evolving vocations.

A major addition was added at the rear of the building on Jeanne-Mance at one point; and repairs made to the exterior—the dome, cornices, and entrances have recently been repaired and painted—back to their original green (from the ugly brown!).

The immediate neighbourhood, predominently Jewish in the 1920s, 1930s, and 1940s, is now a mix of nationalities—French, Portuguese, Italian, and a smaller proportion of Jews. We were told that younger Jewish families are slowly moving back to this area, now considered trendy.

Neighbours had noticed the Star of David on the front of the building and wondered what the building was about. Sue has been advising them—her interest is both personal and historical.

The Best News!

Sue Bronson is working closely with Parks Canada and some members of Montreal's Jewish community to have the Montefiore Home designated as a National Historic Site of Canada.

Their Web site tells us that "Each ... site tells its own unique story, part of the greater story of Canada, contributing a sense of time, identity, and place to our understanding of Canada as a whole ... to commemorate sites, persons, and events associated with ethnocultural communities other than the French and British ..."

We'll keep you posted!

Foster Care

By the time both orphanages had closed, one alternative had been put in place in the early 1940s—foster care became available, and it was less expensive to send children there than to maintain an orphanage.

For many, the foster care experience was horrendous. For Helen Clark, it was good.

> My name is Helen Riva (Shulman) Clark. I was born in Montreal at the Jewish General Hospital in 1936. My parents were Solomon and Rosalind (Kaufmann) Shulman. Over the years, I attended many schools (eight) due to living here and there. Almost like being a gypsy.
>
> I was not an orphan and did not live in either of the orphanages. [However, her aunts, the Wyne sisters, were all in the early Montreal Home on Evans Street. See the biographies for more on the Wyne sisters.] I did live, however, in a foster home for three years, because when I was eight years old, my parents separated. I was left in the custody of my father. He was not equipped to take me at the time and it was arranged through the Baron de Hirsch Institute to place me in a foster home.
>
> In 1944 I went to live with Lionel Levy, his wife Bertha, and children, Shirley and Richard. Richard was about four years older than I was. Shirley about seven years. There was another girl there as well. I think she was two years older than I and her first name was Rosie. Don't remember her last name.
>
> In my last year there, Rosie left and Eleanor Geffin (not sure of her name) came to stay. In a small room off the kitchen we girls had shared a bed and a small armoire with drawers and a place for hanging clothes.
>
> The Levy home was located in a flat on de L'Épée Street in Outremont. I lived there for three years. The Levys were a kind and loving family. We girls were included in their family celebrations such as Passover and Richard's bar mitzvah. We also were able to spend the summers in the Laurentians.
>
> Before living there, I lived on Wiseman Avenue (facing the municipal park), attending Guy Drummond School. After mov-

ing, I switched to Alfred Joyce School on Hutchison and Fairmount streets, where I attended grades three, four, and five.

One summer I attended Sunshine Camp (1948) for the whole season. Most of the children came to stay for only two weeks. I enjoyed the camp but one of the things I didn't like about it was swimming in the leech-infested lake. They had to put plenty of lime in the water when it was time to swim. Also, no parents were allowed to visit. I did see my father once because he had to take me to the orthodontist.

After leaving the Levys', my father and I lived with family. I attended and boarded at Stanstead College when I was fifteen and sixteen years old. Although it was a United Church of Canada school, there were children of other faiths. I have been friends ever since with a Jewish girl I met there.

I now live in the small Ontario town of Fergus with my second husband. I have two girls who each have one son. One lives in the States and the other in Montreal.

Montefiore Hebrew Orphans' Home Alumni

Young men of the Montefiore Home (Back row) unknown, Jack Jacobson, Harry Lenetsky, Harry Zelfin, Charles Bloom, unknown, unknown, Abe Tolmasky, unknown; (Middle row) Jack Spinner, unknown, Willie Bloom, unknown, unknown, unknown, Harry Greenberg, unknown; (Front row) Eli Lenetsky, Norm Bydoff, unknown, Willie Label.

Louis B. Daniels as a 1928 Board member of the Montreal Hebrew Old Peoples' Home. An orginal founder and president of the Montefiore Home.

His grandson today, Edward Daniels, holding a Kiddish Cup presented to his grandfather on May 25, 1933, by the directors of the Montefiore Hebrew Orphans' Home, on his sixtieth birthday in appreciation of his many valuable services on behalf of the orphans of the home.

Dr. A. Bernard Illievitz, medical director, Montefiore Home

Mr. Scholem Lerner, lehrer (teacher) at the Montefiore Home in the 1930s

Mr. A.M. Vineberg, president of the Hebrew Orphans' and Sheltering Home

From the *Canadian Jewish Chronicle*, April 28, 1916, page 1

Abraham Raginsky, first vice-president of the Montefiore Home (1929)

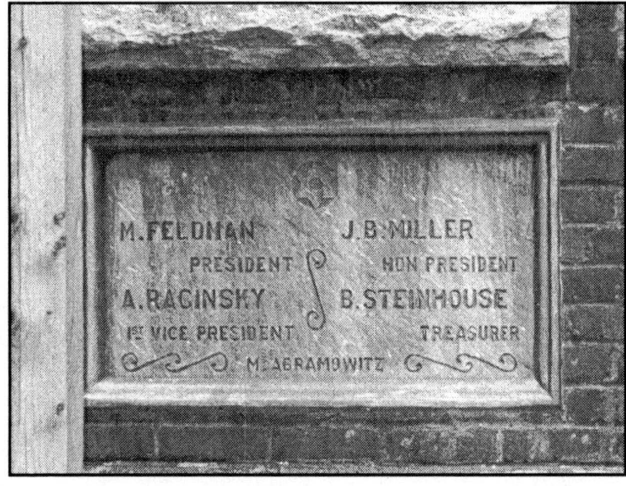

Plaque on front wall of 4650 Jeanne Mance, with names of the board of directors, including A. Raginsky

Alexander Raginsky, president of Dominion Bedding Co. (1935)—the son of Abraham Raginsky

Front steps of the Montefiore Home, filled with parents, kids and volunteers—note the sign written in Yiddish instead of the usual Hebrew.

(Above) Gertrude Raginsky, at far left, with arm around orphan, with staff and summer campers

(Right) husband Alexander, and some happy orphans (1924)

(Far left) Camp cook; (Above) Campers—recognize any?

(Above left) The late 1930s: Arnold Golub, Jack Spinner, Issie Rosenberg, Sam Kaufman;

(Above right) (1930) On Mount Royal (Montreal's famed mountain) Harry Lenetsky, unknown,

Al (Abe) Sheiner, Harry (surname unknown)

(Left) Just hanging around: Abe Sokoloff, Herbie Rasminsky, Hymie Jacobson, Myer G., and Sam Ansell (front) in front of the old Arena Building (circa 1940)

(Left)
Moe Letnick,
2002

(Above) Beautiful
Annie Greenberg,
from Ottawa

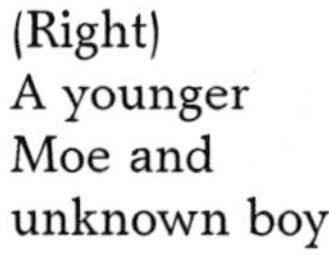

(Right)
A younger
Moe and
unknown boy

(1947) Morris Schneiderman, a dedicated President of the Montefiore Home in the 1930s. He owned the $0.05–$1.00 chain. Pictured here with his first grandson. (Right) In the 1960s. He passed away in 1968 at the age of 77.

Bar Mitzvahed in groups. This celebration in the Montefiore Home (1934) Myer Gordon, Benny Garber, Earl Greenberg, Norman Bydoff, Abe Sokoloff

Most of the Montreal Home Bar Mitzvahs were held at the Shaar Hashomayim Synagogue

(Right) Myer, age 13, and Mom Reva Gordon in 1934

(Left) (Top row) Ben and Toby Gordon (middle row) Ben's kids, Gertie & Mordy; (front row) Myer and his kids, Marilyne and Alan (1959)

Mary Sokoloff, Celia Wiseman, Vita Shein (1941)

(Left) Tina (Celia Wiseman) and Leonard Rosen's 50th anniversary party, 2000, with their family

(Left) Hershel "Harry" and kid brother Eli Lenetsky

(Below) Harry's family came to one of the reunions, with second wife, Rebecca (centre)

(Left) Abie Sokoloff and Hymie Jacobson—1939 vintage (Below) Jack and Hy Jacobson and Max Matt at a 90s reunion

DATE ....

IN GRATEFULLY ACKNOWLEDGING THE RECEIPT OF YOUR KIND CONTRIBUTION WE TAKE OCCASION TO THANK YOU FOR YOUR GENEROUS SUPPORT.

WE CAN ASSURE YOU THAT THIS YOUR VALUABLE FRIENDSHIP WILL SERVE AS A STIMULUS TO OUR DEVOTED FRIENDS TO CONTINUE THEIR BENEVOLENT LABOR IN BEHALF OF OUR POOR AND HOMELESS CHILDREN.

WE NEED MEMBERS, DONORS AND SUBSCRIBERS TO OUR DAILY AND HOURLY SUPPORT STSTEM. URGE YOUR FRIENDS TO JOIN OUR RANKS. SUCH WORK WILL BE VERY MUCH APPRECIATED.

AMOUNT $..................

BOARD OF DIRECTORS,
MONTEFIORE HEBREW ORPHANS' HOME,
1606 MANCE ST.

(Left) Pre-1926 donor card, submitted by Montreal archivist Eiran Harris. Note: the word system is mispelled.

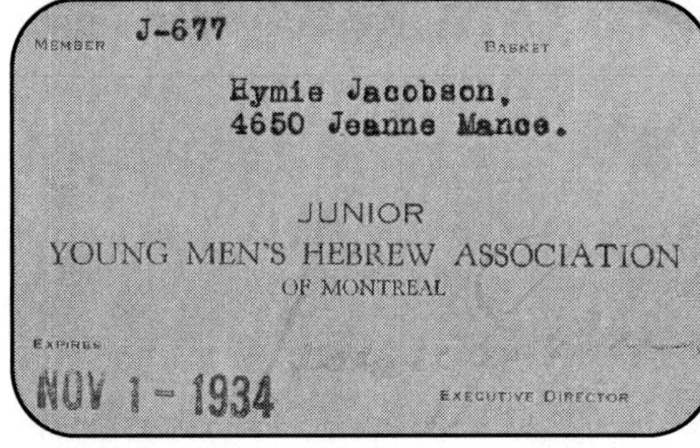

MEMBER J-677 BASKET

Hymie Jacobson,
4650 Jeanne Mance.

JUNIOR
YOUNG MEN'S HEBREW ASSOCIATION
OF MONTREAL

EXPIRES
NOV 1 - 1934

EXECUTIVE DIRECTOR

(Left) Hymie Jacobson's pass for the YMHA, built circa 1931

Below is one of Manny Cohen's prize possessions from the past. This letter was given to him by Principal Maravei. He attended Bancroft School before he went into the Montreal Home in Westmount in 1938, following the death of his mother, Ida.

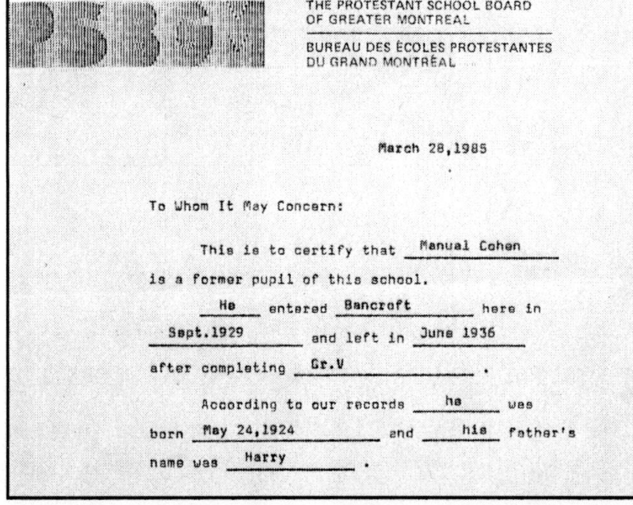

PSBGM

THE PROTESTANT SCHOOL BOARD
OF GREATER MONTREAL

BUREAU DES ÉCOLES PROTESTANTES
DU GRAND MONTRÉAL

March 28,1985

To Whom It May Concern:

This is to certify that Manual Cohen is a former pupil of this school.

He entered Bancroft here in Sept.1929 and left in June 1936 after completing Gr.V.

According to our records he was born May 24,1924 and his father's name was Harry.

AN EXCITING 2003 REUNION

Why was this reunion different from all other reunions? Because it was planned around three of our book events. Our usual Saturday night dinner was the only segment just for the alumni. Over forty people gathered at Montreal's Le Biftheque, patiently waiting for its five Toronto attendees to arrive, not only for our company but also for the nibbles we were bringing with us. Luckily for them, the restaurant supplied something and when we ran in, panting and forty-five minutes late, our dragged-from-Toronto appetizers weren't greeted with much enthusiasm.

Fortunately, *we* were! The conversation was warm and wonderful, reminiscent as usual; the food was always delicious and plentiful (which necessitated a few doggy bags), and the evening was topped off with our guest from CBC Radio One, host Loreen Pindera, who was there as part of her weekend blitz to capture our words and mood for posterity, or at least for her radio listeners on two upcoming shows that coming week. Some alumni brought guests; Manny Cohen brought his son.

We bid goodnight by 10:30, with plans to meet for our special Sunday event, an alumni breakfast co-hosted in, and by, the Cummings Jewish Centre for Seniors, and the Jewish Public Library, followed by a *read* of *Four Hundred Brothers and Sisters* by its author and her Montefiore Home alumnus spouse! This was open to the public, and they responded positively, filling the auditorium.

The talk was well received, with many questions and comments from the floor. Among them was alumnus Jack Miller, not seen nor heard from in over ten years, and others, such as Teddy Naiman, who thought they might have been in one of the homes yet not quite sure, and Sam Schwartz—now a Florida resident—who was so delighted to have been with us that day. A beautiful bouquet of flowers was presented to Judy, who in turn presented a cheque for

$1,000 to Susan Karpman, acting director of Jewish Family Services, the first instalment of many more to come, gleaned from the profits of books sold. Thanks were extended to the Gordons by Dr. Karin Doerr.

The next morning, CBC host Loreen arranged for four Montefiore alumni—Myer Gordon, Earl Greenberg, Ida Sklar Lewis, and Vita Shein Seidler, who had attended Bancroft School while in the home—to meet with current Bancroft students, grades 3 to 6. Joining in was their former supervisor, Max Matt, ninety-three years young in December 2003, and his sister Hilda Brownstone, a Montreal Home alumna, plus two Montreal Home alumni, Murial Fishman and Judge Irving Pfeffer.

They went from class to class with an entourage of teachers, principal Arty Maravei, author Judy, and several others: Loreen; Ida's daughter Marlene; Mike Cohen, the *Suburban* and *English Montreal School Board* columnist; and Saul Pfeffer, Irving's first cousin. Saul hadn't seen Irving since the latter dropped in on his way overseas during World War II—sixty years earlier!—to visit him and his mother.

The alumni talked with the children, comparing the school then and now, and answering a slew of questions from *today's kids*. Of all questions they could ask, the most outstanding (and surprising) one, addressed to Hilda, was: "How old are you?" She didn't hesitate a minute to answer, "Eighty-seven." The kids were amazed!

Judge Pfeffer, now living in San Francisco, California, was a great role model for the kids because he told them his story of long years of study even after his teachers had discouraged him from going beyond public school, saying he wasn't smart enough. He spoke of the importance of working hard and doing your best. It certainly worked for him! He can now plead cases before the United States Supreme Court! Always great to meet someone who started from nothing and went on to great things, alumnus or not!

Far from being an almost all Jewish school as it was in the 20s and 30s, the students came from every walk of life and were every colour, with seemingly only two Jewish teachers (who both bought our book!). What they all had in common was the smile on their faces. And what well-disciplined, polite, eager, interested kids—what a pleasurable experience it was! They treated us like royalty, with delicious refreshments and a gift for each alumni—note cards with beautiful drawings done by the youngsters themselves. These cards are one of the school's fundraising projects and are sold to help buy much-needed equipment.

The Gordons made a presentation of *Four Hundred Brothers and Sisters* to Principal Maravei. The book has a home in the school library and serves as a reference for today's students to read about others with whom they share some experiences, though the latter went to the school over seventy years ago.

While talking with the principal, she revealed some school secrets—the salaries of teachers and principals of that era, that is, in 1933: The dedicated, and still well-remembered principal, after working thirty-five years with very few absences, earned about $4,200. A teacher, after twenty-four years of service, earned about $1,200! They were all truly dedicated then.

As a comparison, a personal friend of the Gordons has a sister who was a teacher in the early 1950s—her annual salary in the *early years* was $2,000. It seems the teaching profession had to wait until unions became involved in the education system for salaries to rise with the times.

And to top it off, Principal Maravei had also gotten the report cards of the four school alumni—they had done pretty well! Records of hundreds (or probably thousands) of former Bancroft School pupils were printed and handwritten on index cards in a filing cabinet in the back room. One more way for the Bancroft students of today "to get that sense of continuity and history—even these old people were once students who had to worry about report cards," said Loreen, who was recording the whole morning for her radio program.

* * *

Principal Maravei also handed out copies of the following from the Edmonton Public School System. Can you believe some of these rules?!

Rules for Teachers, 1915

1. You will not marry during the term of your contract.
2. You are not to keep company with men.
3. You must be home between the hours of 8 p.m. and 6 a.m. unless attending a school function.
4. You may not loiter downtown in ice cream stores.
5. You may not travel beyond the city limits unless you have the permission of the Chairman of the Board.
6. You may not ride in a carriage or automobile with any man unless he is your father or your brother.
7. You may not smoke cigarettes.
8. You may not dress in bright colours.
9. You may under no circumstances dye your hair.
10. You must wear at least two petticoats.
11. Your dresses must not be any shorter than two inches above the ankle.
12. To keep the school room neat and clean, you must:
    Sweep the floor at least twice daily.
    Scrub the floor at least once a week with hot, soapy water.
    Clean the blackboards at least once a day and start the fire at 7 a.m. so the room will be warm by 8 a.m.

Because of the not-so-perfect quality of the writing on the report cards, I am taking the liberty of re-typing the information from Myer Gordon's three cards—after a fashion—but you get the idea; no one else wanted to share their marks! But what an amazing thing for today's seniors to grasp in their hands, and such fun reading!

No.	Family Name	Given Name	Born	Religion
4543	Gordon	Myer	21/1/21	J

Address	Parent	Entered here
4650 Mance	Morris	4/2/27

Half-Year Ending	Grade	Room	Half-Year Ending	Grade	Room
June 1927	1–1	[3 a.m.]	Jan. 1932	5–2	28
Jan. 1928	1–2	[7 p.m.]	June 1932	5–1	25
June 1928	2–1	[3 p.m.]	Jan. 1933	6–1	33
Jan. 1929	2–2	[8 p.m.]	June 1934	7–1	33
June 1929	3–1	21	Jan. 1934	7–2	32
Jan. 1930	3–2	11	June 1934	7–1	32
June 1930	4–1	12	Jan. 1935	7–1	26
Jan. 1931	4–2	23	June 1935	7–2	32
June 1931	5–1	28			

Half-Year Ending	Grade	Per cent in Tests Arith.	Eng.	Spell.	Total %	Days Abs.	Times Late
June '27	1–1	G				7	
Jan. '28	1–	G				8	3
June '28	2–1	G		G		3	0
Jan. '29	2–2	28/28	F	30/30		10	
June '29	3–1	66/75		74/75		5 1/2	0
Jan. '30	3–2	82	38/50	47		2	0
June '30	4–1	72	75	69		2	0
Jan. '31	4–2	80	67	72	66.1	12 1/2	0
June '31	5–1	78	63	94	72	7	0
Jan. '32	5–2	78	69.6	80	63.8	14	1
June '32	5–2	90		46/50	76	7 1/2	0
Jan. '33	6–1	84/100	85/125	49/50	71.8	16	0
June '33	6–2	59/100	81/125	46/50	55.8	31	0
Jan. '34	6–2	75	124	48	71	3	0
June '34	7–1					25	
Jan. '35	7–2	44/60	65/100	[a]	39.1	13	0
June '35	7–2	69	150/225	French 49	65.6	3 1/2	0

In June 1932, Myer received first place honours in Reading, Gymnastics, Arithmatic and Manual Training!

The reunion continues ...

As noted before, Sue Bronson loved to tell the city, country, and the world about historical Montreal. She's charming, knowledgeable, capable, and *so-o-o-o-o* willing to share!

When we first met her in August 2002, she took us over to the Montefiore Home (remember, she lives across the street), introduced us to some staff of the French daycare, now housed there, and to some of the parents, who spoke a very limited English. And they all bought our book—the initial print hot off the presses—how wonderful! She had now arranged for us to do a *read* for her group in conjunction with the September 2003 MHOH reunion.

What was even more exciting was that the event was held in the basement of this former Montefiore Home and was attended not only by the Mile End Memories members, but also by neighbours on the street and some of the home's alumni. Our MC was Aldo Marchini, former CBC host. As we talked, the building became alive with the memories of these former residents. Some of the alumni joined us on stage. While sharing their memories, they could look around the room and relate how the dining room benches and tables were set up in rows and point to the kitchen in the back. But the pantry was in the front—strange by today's layouts for convenience! Supervisor Max Matt also had an office between the dining room and kitchen. The lower room was now a playroom.

Sue's niece, Samie Marshy, a former pupil in the daycare and now a teenager, coloured a poster of the building and presented it to us in the form of a plaque, containing the public relations blurb advertising the event. Afterwards, everyone enjoyed coffee and cookies. And—the *kids* who once lived there were given a special tour of the building. Emotions were high, tears were running, chatter was non-stop. What an evening!

In discussions with Sue, it was arranged that the main floor foyer would be the site of a plaque recognizing the building as a Jewish orphanage, and most importantly, recognizing all the children who lived there. This plaque was to be unveiled during the September 2004 reunion weekend.

* * *

Joe Fiorito has a way with words ...

In this interview with *Toronto Star* columnist, Joe Fiorito, which was published in the September 19, 2003, edition entitled: *Kibitzing and kvelling over coffee with Myer, Earl, Sam and Sylvia: Jewish orphans still feel the pain ...*, he captures the feelings, the still-raw emotions of the four alumni.

> Myer Gordon and his pal Earl Greenberg had a cup of coffee with Sam and Sylvia Rasminsky the other day. The four friends live in North York. They see each other socially now and then. They like to tell the old stories and look at the old photos and share a few old jokes. Myer, who is in his eighties, is a card. He says, "I can do ten minutes stand-up. And an hour lying down."
>
> Better to laugh than to cry. They are the Jewish orphans.
>
> You stop being an orphan when you're old enough to vote or drive a car or go to war or find a girl and fall in love and have a family of your own. They have done all these things long ago. Some of these things they have done many times over.
>
> But memories of childhood grow sharper over time, and the four friends share a keen and specific bond: they were Jewish orphans during the Depression, which was a lousier time than usual to be without parents; and aren't Jewish families supposed to look after their own? Life happens, not always neatly.
>
> Sam says, "I was nine when I went in. My mother, I remember her in bed, sick. I don't remember anything else. And then my father died. He was a poker player. He owned a valet service. He died at the poker table on New Year's Eve. This was 1931. They put us in the orphanage."
>
> Earl says, "There were six of us. My father was an invalid. My mother passed away when I was five. My older sister stayed and looked after my dad. The rest of us ended up in the home."
>
> Myer says, "My father died when I was two years and ten months old. When I was five and a half, I went in.
>
> My mother was American. She moved back to the States to get work. She said, "I'll come back." She came back a year later. She said, "I want my boys." They said, "Take Benny, leave Myer here." So I spent nine more years in the orphanage. We lived in a world of our own.

Sylvia says, "I didn't know anyone on the other side of that high fence." Sam says, "The Jewish public didn't know we existed. It might be because they were embarrassed." He pauses to consider. He doesn't want to give the wrong impression. He adds, "I'm just guessing."

Myer says, "I kvell—I nearly cry—every day. My mother visited me in ten years five times." He kvells to think of it. "She would send me a couple of bucks to buy malted milk." Sam says, "You were holding out on me. I never got any of that malted milk."

Earl says, "I ran away once. I wanted to see my dad. He was living in Ottawa. I was thirteen or fourteen. I took the train. It cost two bucks. I had the fare because I had a part-time job assembling lamps. My father was living in a kind of lean-to. No plumbing. I don't know what was the matter with him. I guess he had cancer. I think about him every day of my life." And he, too, kvells.

Sylvia, who met Sam in the orphanage, says, "My grandfather was a scribe in Poland. He wrote the Torahs. He came to Canada first. It took six years for him to bring us over. My father died a year later of an aneurysm. My mother got peritonitis from a burst appendix. The youngest went to live with my grandmother. Three of us went to the orphanage."

She landed lightly, in a way. There were two Jewish orphanages. One was much better off than the other. Sylvia says, "We had elocution lessons. We had piano. We had a skating rink in winter. And we even had Irving Layton. He was with us for a year or so as a supervisor." She pauses and says, almost guiltily, "I lived a life of privilege. We had a nurse, and a hospital floor with two wards. We had a dentist, and a barber came to do our hair. We went to summer camp."

That sounds pretty swell, until she gives it a twist. "When the home closed, children who had one parent went to live with that parent. I went to my mother. She lived in an unheated flat. There was ice along the baseboards. I sat on the floor and I cried. I was with my mother. But I was unhappy. It took a long time to get over it."

Sam says, "You didn't get over it." Myer says, "We won't get over it."

And they kvell, and so do I.

The thirteenth combined reunion of the Jewish orphans took place this weekend in Montreal. It is the fourteenth such event. Myer and his wife, Judy, are the main organizers. They always make sure there are plenty of boxes of tissues on all the tables at the dinner. The orphans consider that they are each other's brothers and sisters; fewer of them every year.

Many more reasons to kvell.

Joe was enchanted with the whole idea of this story, and upon finishing the interview, shook his head in wonder and said, "With all of your experiences and amazing mental and physical health, you are a society unto yourselves."

Reunions over the years

1989 First Reunion: Hugs and tears were everywhere, as shown by Tina (Celia Wiseman) Rosen and Evelyn (Shano) Furlong. Evelyn died several months later, Tina in 2002

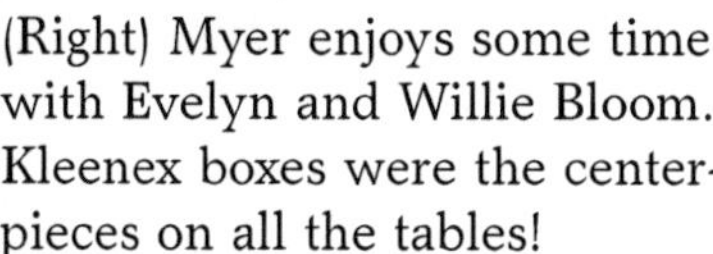

(Right) Myer enjoys some time with Evelyn and Willie Bloom. Kleenex boxes were the centerpieces on all the tables!

(Left) Jack and Rose Senderoff, visited by the Gordons in their Florida home, circa 1999; (Below) Harry and Marilyn Miller; Montefiore Home

(Above) Dave & Daisy Cherry at '89 reunion (Right) Abe Sheiner presents former supervisor Max Matt with a plaque at our first reunion

(Left) Mike Mendelson and Louis Bloom, early 90s reunion.

(Below) Circa 1997, Ida Lewis, Willie Label, Vita Seidler, Mamie and Sam Pap (Mamie's first husband Max Milstein was in the Montefiore Home), Rebecca Lenetsky (widow of Harry), Moe Adelstein

Brothers get together at the 1995 reunion. (Back row) Myer Gordon, Louis Brumer, Saul Tolmasky, John Brownston, Manny Cohen, Earl Greenberg, Harry Schwartz, Joe Miller; (Front row) Harry Lenetsky, Sam Rasminsky, Max Matt, Nathan Cohen

(Right) Herb and Sam Rasminsky

(Left) Joining us at the 1994 reunion: Sylvia Savitsky and Sam Rasminsky brought their five beautiful daughters—who gave them many grandsons!

Reunion boat tour around Montreal Island, 2002. Enjoying the scenery are Irma and Lester Dick, and Judge Irving Pfeffer; Montreal Home

(Right) Esther Goldfarb and Saul Tolmasky

(Below) Moe and Jeannine Adelstein, Jack Zukerman and Rose, Charles Berman, unknown, and Myer Gordon—a mix of both homes at a '90s reunion.

(Above) Our only Florida reunion, February 1993:
Max Matt, Arnold Golub, Ruth Furman, Gertie Golub,
David Furman

(Below) Alice & Joe Miretsky, Arnold & Gert (Miretsky)
Golub, at same event

(Above) Hy Jacobson, Saul Tolmasky, Abe Tolmasky, Myer Gordon, Dave Cherry, Max Matt, Willie Bloom; (kneeling) Sammy Ticker, 1989

(Below) Willie Label and Sylvia, Bess Alper, Rebecca Lenetsky, Nat Alper, alumni reunion

The Birth of a Book

The first book is sold at the August 2002 reunion in Montreal! Joining in on the excitement are Janice Arnold, reporter for the *Canadian Jewish News*, and Eiran Harris, archivist, Jewish Public Library, Montreal.

Forever trying to sell books at any and all Jewish book fairs!

(Left) At our book launch, Toronto Jewish Book Fair, November 2002. Earl Greenberg, Myer Gordon, Vita Seidler, Judy Gordon, with granddaughter Jordana Asch. A proud day for all!

(Above) Our interview with *Toronto Star* columnist Joe Fiorito, August 2003. Sylvia and Sam Rasminsky, Joe, Earl and Sandy Greenberg, Myer and Judy Gordon.

(Right) Judge Irving Pfeffer and *Montreal Gazette* reporter Ann McLaughlin at the 1990 reunion

(Below left) Saul & Dorothy White visit with the Gordons at the 2002 Montreal Jewish Book Fair.

(Below right) At the Ottawa Book Fair, Spring '02, with Bea Hock

Presentation by the Gordons of *Four Hundred Brothers and Sisters* to students and principal of Bancroft School, with old and 'new' pupils! September 2003: MHOH Alumni Vita Seidler, Ida Lewis, student, Principal Arty Maravei, Earl Greenberg, student, Myer and Judy Gordon, author. (Left) The changing faces of Bancroft.

(Left) The Gordons flank Earl and Sandy Greenberg at a meeting with archivist Eiran Harris.

Eiran 'found' many of the historical illustrations and articles in this book. What a helpful and nice person!

(Right) At the September 2003 reunion, the Gordons present the first Alumni donation from book sales to Susan Karpman, acting director, Montreal's Jewish Family Services.

(Right) Our elder statesmen, Max Matt and Max Alper watch as the author signs Book One—hot off the presses—at the 2002 reunion.

(Left) Myer poses with our Montefiore Club hosts: Rachel Alkallay, program, and Susan Stern, president, October 2003.

(Right) Myer with Dov Okouneff, documentary filmmaker, who added a seven-minute segment about Myer and the homes in a remake of his 1930s *Montreal's Jewish Memories*. He taped this segment at the Montefiore Club.

(Below) Stanley Abbey, son of the late Monroe, has questions following the Gordons' talk at The Montefiore Club, Montreal. Monroe Abbey was among the many Westmounters who served on the Board of the Montreal Hebrew Orphans' Home on Claremont Avenue

(Right) Janice Rosen, director, Canadian Jewish Congress National Archives, accepts some MHOH alumni archives to keep there for all to view, September 2003

Max and his girls: These photos are good marketing tools, showing happy alumni with their beloved Montefiore Home supervisor! Max Matt and his girls. (Above left: Ida Lewis and Sophie Kazdan, circa 1996; (Above right) Helen Zawalsky, Sylvia Rasminsky, and Tina Rosen; (Front) Vita Seidler (1994 reunion).

ALUMNI BIOGRAPHIES

Remembering Their Brothers and Sisters

The oldest group of children had to graduate or leave at the age of sixteen. They went to live with family, friends, in foster homes, or their own apartments. Or they went to the arenas of World War II. However, they continued to return to the homes to give encouragement to the *kids*—taking them to the movies, just playing with them, or joining them at summer camp.

There was no organized alumni group until the mid-1950s, and after 1989, the combined alumni began to get together in earnest, talking over their past and current lives, comparing notes and memories. The following biographies fill us in on some of the details.

Moe Adelstein and Min Adelstein Leibovitch

MIN'S TRIBUTE TO THE MONTEFIORE HEBREW ORPHANS' HOME

My brother, Moe, was eight years old, and I was only five when our mother died. Our father found it very difficult to work and take care of us at the same time. After discussing the situation with relatives and friends, he made the decision to place us in the Montefiore Home.

The two years we lived in the home were a blessing. Compassionate Max Matt and his staff were as close and as good as real family could be.

Dad married again. He and our stepmother, Shaindel, set up a home to include Moe and me. The two years of kind and caring family-type life we had in the home made the transition to our parents' home very easy.

I attended two reunions of our brothers and sisters. The first reunion ... in Montreal, was very emotional for me. To see my brothers and sisters, after so many years, was overwhelming. I had the same feeling at the reunion that was held in Toronto.

I am happily married to Hy Leibovitch (a.k.a. "Leibo") and live in Edmonton. We have three sons and one daughter. Two of our sons and daughter are married. G-d has blessed us with eleven grandchildren and one great grandchild, *kein-ein-horah*.

Thank you very much for sending me the newsletters. I will always be interested in reading about, and keeping up with the news of, my brothers and sisters."

* * *

Henry Albert

MONTREAL HOME

Henry was put in the Montreal Hebrew Orphans' Home in 1920, along with his sister Mamie and his brothers Leo and Julius. His mother had died and his father had to put four of his five children into the home. When the deadly fire of 1922 destroyed the summer camp in Shawbridge, Julius, the eldest, bravely picked up younger brother Henry and carried him out of the fire.

When Julius turned sixteen in 1927 and had to leave the home (according to the rules), their father said all had to leave—he wanted to keep his kids together. They moved in with an uncle—six people and two beds. As crowded as life was, sharing was still an important value to the family. Another orphan, Herbie Rose—who came out of the home at about the same time (see his bio under Annie Rosenbaum)—was allowed to sleep on the floor.

Henry recently sent the Gordons a scrap of paper with the following song, *his* song, but written, crudely in red ink, by a staff member. He was seven or eight at the time.

Glorious and True to the Dear H.O.H. *

Where forever we may roam,
far from our childhood home,
Glorious and true to the dear H.O.H.
Enshrined in our memory,
fair shalt thou ever be.

* * *

* *Hebrew Orphans' Home.*

Connie Bercusson Gore

MONTEFIORE HOME

A Child's Destiny

Everything was so pleasant. I was a young child of eight with loving parents and an older brother who was fourteen. We were a happy family and had lots of fun. My mother was a very pretty lady, and my father—he was my hero. I was their little princess who had everything. I can remember coming home from school one day to find a new phonograph (which was rare in those days) playing a record for me called *Three Little Words, I Love You*. I always looked forward to coming home to find my mother there waiting for me.

Then one afternoon, my whole world collapsed. When I arrived home, I was told that my mother had become very ill and was taken to the hospital. I never saw her again because she died a few weeks later due to an ear infection. There was no penicillin at the time. She was thirty-seven years old, and I was eight.

After a short period, my father hired a housekeeper to look after us. She was very ugly and had flaming red hair. I've disliked anyone with red hair ever since. However, my father seemed to find her attractive and married her a few months later. She also convinced him to make a will leaving her as the sole beneficiary should he pass away.

What a cruel stepmother she turned out to be. She abused me and locked me in a dark closet for hours. I was petrified of her. Finally, my father felt he could no longer subject me to her abuse and placed me in an orphanage. I was very lonely and frightened. I wanted to go back home, but there was no home for me to go to. My stepmother would not have me there.

After several months, I adjusted to being in the orphanage. I can remember some good and bad things about it. My fondest memory is meeting Earl Greenberg. He was so sweet and kind, which helped me to overcome my fears of being there. Each child was also given a *big sister* to care for her. Mine was Esther Gold, who was all of four years older than I was. She was also a wonderful person.

My brother was allowed to remain in the house with my father and stepmother because she seemed to like him. I guess he presented no threat to her. One year after my father married her, he died suddenly. I was told he was overfed and died of acute indigestion.

I remained in the orphanage for another year, when, at last, an aunt agreed to have me live with her. I was taken from one aunt to another for the next few years. Finally a very poor aunt agreed to keep me. She barely had enough money to feed her own children, but she accepted me and treated me as one of her own. She made me a part of a family again. She welcomed my friends and taught me humility and kindness by her own good deeds.

At the age of fifteen, I had to leave school and go to work to help pay for my keep. All my aunts did not think it was necessary for me to continue school.

Many years have passed since all this happened. I am indeed grateful to have a wonderful husband, five children who are all married now, and ten grandchildren. I inspired my children to further their education and each one has achieved a successful professional career. At this time I also returned to school and graduated with a college degree in social sciences.

I carry no bitterness about losing my parents at such a young age, but instead I like to think that my life experiences have contributed to my being a better person and have given me a sense of compassion toward others and especially toward other young unfortunate children.

As I reflect back, perhaps I would have been happier had I remained in the orphanage instead of being moved from one aunt to another. Both my parents passed away within two years of each other, so I was deprived of belonging anywhere and of being one of this big family of brothers and sisters.

However, who knows which may have been the better way.

* * *

Edie Bye

MONTREAL HOME

My parents came from New York to Montreal to be the supervisors at the Montreal (Westmount) Home in 1926, where they remained until the facility closed in 1942. My brother, Abe, and I lived with them in the apartment they were given, right in the home itself.

I went to Herbert Simons Public School in N.D.G. I played with the orphaned children and had many friends. I attend all the alumni reunions because it gives me a chance to meet again with my old friends.

I especially liked the Jewish holidays when we would dress up in new clothing—I loved the new dresses! I also liked skating outside at the home and enjoyed the music the kids were privileged to hear every week.

* * *

David Cherry

MONTEFIORE HOME

Dave was born on September 9, 1916, and was put into the Montefiore Home with his brother Harry and sister Rose after his mother died, about 1923. When their father remarried in 1930, the children went back home—soon after Dave's bar mitzvah. It is interesting to note that their new stepmother was mother to the Wagon children, other orphans also in the home. Together they could take their children out to make one happy family.

Dave was in the army and then became a dress cutter, working for a company for many years. Eventually, he opened his own business and married Daisy. They both made it to the 1989 reunion, but poor health has kept them away since.

* * *

Herb Cohen

MONTREAL HOME: 1935–1941

I was very young, about six years old, when my mother died giving birth to my youngest sister. I had two other sisters older than I, and I guess my father could not cope with four children, especially a newborn. He placed my sister Josephine (now deceased) and I in the orphanage at that time. She was about two years older than I.

My first memories are of the administrator, a kindly old white-haired gent, and his wife. I can't recall his name, but I wasn't frightened at all. I can't recall the earliest years of my stay; the memories that do come out must be from later years when I must have been about seven or eight years old.

I must say that I have only good memories from my stay there. There always seemed to be things to do. Many were inventions of the kids there. One game I do recall vividly was called *tipee*. This was played in what I think was the gym—played using a small stick about six to eight inches long, pointed at both ends. With a longer stick, it was hit on any end and flipped in the air to be smacked with the big stick. There was also skating in the winter. I recall my father brought a pair of skates on visiting day, and my sister and I fought over who would have them.

I remember one of the counsellors, named Ogulnick (always referred as "Oggie" behind his back—actually he was a supervisor). He was quite the tough one as I recall, and he did give me a hard time once in a while, like sending me to the basement with the laundry at night, all by myself. I was terrified of the dark then. I guess I might have deserved it at that time.

Another great time was Halloween, when most of the kids would climb out the windows to go trick-or-treating. In Westmount, we got the greatest candies there. Don't recall anyone being caught, so maybe they knew and let us have some fun.

The best time, of course, was summer, when we went to Sunshine Camp. I can never forget some of the great times there, such as the treasure hunts, campfires, baseball games, and, of course, the swimming! I learned to swim properly there. I recall diving to the bottom to retrieve plates, as part of a test, and then swimming from the shore to the raft a number of times with all the kids cheering. It was always a sad time when camp was over and we went back to the city and school.

One year there were auditions to sing in the choir at the Shaar Hashomayim Synagogue, and I was lucky enough to be one of those chosen. That was also great, because we walked there every Saturday for the services, after which there was always a Kiddush, with great food and drinks. The choir was always included. I sang in the choir for about four years, and today I still recall some of the music when I am in synagogue.

In 1941 my Father had remarried, and so was forced to take us back home. It was kind of sad to leave, because I was quite happy there and had made many friends. I still sang in the choir for about a year afterwards, but was then asked to leave because I had problems travelling there from where we lived, and they also wished to give another of the boys a chance to sing.

I think that the image of orphanages, in many places, was misunderstood. I believe the MHOH gave me some of the best years of my early life, and without it, many of the boys would not have turned out as successful as most of us did.

* * *

Ben Gordon

MONTEFIORE HOME

Courtesy of daughter, Gertie (Gail)

Ben was a hyper child and was put into a military school when his mother took him back with her to New York City. He moved back with her when she returned to Montreal upon the death of her sister, whereupon she married her brother-in-law—so the six boys (four nephews and her two sons, Ben and Myer) would have a real mother, not a stepmother.

When Ben married Toby Schwartz near the start of World War II, they had time for a three-day honeymoon, and Ben soon left to serve in the army for three years. Son Mordy was born one year after his return and has 3 sons and now a granddaughter of his own; daughter Gert has a son and a daughter.

* * *

Martin Gordon

MONTREAL HOME

These early memories are dedicated to the key players (for Martin) in the home and summer camp: Maurice Ogulnick, Ila Kaufman, Mr. and Mrs. Bye, Mr. Arthur Schalek, Mr. Sydney Levine, Mrs. Kramer, and Mrs. Ticker.

Martin phoned out of the blue in October 2003 to say that he had been in the Montreal (Westmount) Home from around 1937 until it closed in 1942, and had vivid memories of the people in the home and at Sunshine Camp.

Martin was born in 1932 and lost his father to tuberculosis when he was three years old. It was during the Depression and his widowed mother tried her best to keep her family together with odd jobs. But as it got more difficult, she was advised to put Martin into the orphanage until things got better for her.

So, in 1937, he entered the Montreal Home, spending the first week upstairs in the infirmary, and then he was put into a dorm with boys his own age: Irving Levinson, brother of Gerry and Andy; Leon Markson; and Oscar Muchnick, brother of Bessie.

One of his first recollections was being in the basement hallway near the gym and seeing these two cute little girls, his age, heading his way. One had dark hair and eyes, Katy Gold; the other was blond, blue-eyed, and chubby, Annie Reisler. He was then called into the office by the Byes where he met Minnie Engle (an older girl), who was given some money and asked to take him down the hill to Sherbrooke Street for a badly needed haircut.

> As a kid, I had this thick mop of curly (kinky) blonde hair—like an Afro. I think it was Cecil Yanovitch who gave me the nickname *Brushy*—he was a genius at giving kids nicknames! He thought my hair looked like a thick brush. *Brushy* has lasted right up to today; I was seldom called Martin.

Some memories of Berthelet School centre around Moishe Ticker, the son of the cook, Mrs. Ticker. The orphanage kids were often bullied by the *other* kids, but one person was always there to protect them—Moishe Ticker. They could always rely on him for protection! One happy school memory was of the principal, Mr. Bennett, whose greatest delight was showing movies for the school children. He smiled broadly while he put up signs announcing the shows. "Two of my favourites were *The Thirty-nine Steps* and *Mrs. Wiggs and the Cabbage Patch.*" Mr. Bennett acted as projectionist.

Martin also says he vividly remembers Lester Dick's dad at the school bus stop, and he remembers the royal visit to Canada in 1939, when the home kids who were cub scouts saw the king and queen near Mount Royal.

The home closed in 1942, but Martin stayed on for several years at the summer camp.

> Just a note about how I fared as an adult. Showing artistic talent and encouraged by Board member Mr. Gilletz, I gravitated into art courses at the YMHA, the Montreal Museum of Fine Arts, and later, Sir George Williams School of Fine Arts. I became a graphic artist in the sign profession, working at times for others but usually as a freelancer—meeting many people and learning a lot. I soon became pretty good at what I was doing!
>
> My stay at the home was very pleasant. I cherish and appreciate every memory of the kids, the staff, and Sunshine Camp, and I wish to say something of the key players, who were so dedicated to the betterment of the kids. I remember them all with fondness, gratitude, and respect.

Mr. Maurice "Oggie" Ogulnick, Supervisor

> In effect, for me, Oggie *was* the home. He had a small, sparsely furnished room next to the kids' dormitories. They called us Midgets, Inters, and Seniors. His door was always open and kids would come and go in spirited conversation.
>
> One of my earliest memories of him was in the shower room, with washcloth in hand, single-handedly washing and bathing ten or twelve little screaming kids (Midgets) all at the same time. This was one of his duties and responsibilities. He was solely

responsible for fifty boys, aged five to sixteen, some of them *not a gift*.

For those who didn't know or remember Oggie, he was in his late twenties at the time, unmarried—a big-boned guy, well over two hundred pounds, and over 5 feet 10 inches. His sparse hair was neatly groomed, and he wore a small moustache, looking a bit like King Farouk of Egypt. Neatly dressed, but I never saw him in a suit. He was intelligent; full of enthusiasm, self-assurance, and energy; a non-smoker and non-drinker, I believe.

His one weakness was food, of which he consumed large portions. He rarely ate at the staff table, preferring to eat in the downstairs kitchen where he could eat as he pleased in peace! He loved Lime Rickey soft drinks, popular at the time. I often heard him tell a kid, "Be a good boy! Here's some money. Go down to the corner and get me a Lime Ricky!"

In all my years in the home and at camp [contrary to the experiences others wrote about], I never remember him laying a hand on me. He was always respectful and nice to me and always tried to engage me in conversation, asking my opinion and thoughts on ideas—very flattering for a skinny kid of seven or eight years of age. He had a passion for educating his kids on current and world events and how they affected the Jews. Following the outbreak of World War II, he was always looking for ways to help the Allied cause.

I hold this memory as clear as yesterday. One day, passing Oggie's open door, I noticed he was listening intently to the little radio he kept near the window. Suddenly, he gave a loud whoop and turned to me exclaiming, "Germany just invaded Russia. That's good news. Let them fight it out, two less enemies for Britain and the Allies to worry about!"

But sadly, of course, Canada had to declare war the following September, 1939.

He had a sense of humour, and the twinkle in his eye was for others as well as for me. He was down-to-earth, honest, plain, and direct. What you saw was what you got.

Oggie gave his youth to the orphans, and even after he married in the 1950s, he still continued to serve the interests of the Jewish community all his life.

Oggie was very dear to Martin, like Max Matt was to the children of the Montefiore Home.

Miss Ila Kaufman, Girls' Supervisor

> To us kids, boys and girls alike, she was always just "Miss Kaufman." A former resident of the Montreal Home herself, Miss Kaufman, in my time, was in her late twenties, had dark hair and eyes, was quite attractive actually—with a beautiful smile for the kids. Always confident but upbeat, positive, sympathetic, and easy to talk to.
>
> As a little kid, I always thought to marry Miss Kaufman!
>
> Her greatest joy and passion was to teach the boys and girls the arts. Gilbert and Sullivan operettas were very popular in those days, and the children performed many of them under her tutelage, especially at the Sunshine Camp. I can remember, in 1941, Miss Kaufman at the piano near the stage, pecking out the tunes, and boys and girls excitedly gathered around.

Sunshine Camp

Martin presents a colourful description of the camp. He attended from 1938 to 1948, first as a camper, and then as a junior counsellor.

> The balcony wrapped around half the dining room mess hall, overlooking the most gorgeous lake and mountain scenery in the Laurentians. It was built on large logs, about twenty feet up from the rocky shoreline of Lac Masson. With a view of the village too! And of the island and rock on the other side, which the kids called the *Rock of Gibraltar*.
>
> If there ever was a paradise on earth, that had to be Sunshine Camp. Many of the kids wished we could stay and live there forever. One reason was because, as everyone agreed, the best donuts in Canada could be found in a little *boulangerie* in the village of Sainte-Marguerite—for 25 cents a dozen.

Mr. Arthur Schalek, Board Member

> Mr. Schalek was a dynamic and dedicated volunteer at the home and camp. He took his job very seriously. He was rather tall and portly, with grey balding hair, but he looked important. He was

always jolly, approachable, and without pretensions—just the sweetest man, giving and dedicated.

To visualize him, he was a cross between Santa Claus, your favourite uncle, and a P.T. Barnum show biz impresario type!

Mr. Schalek constantly arranged free entertainment, such as movies, skating shows, the circus, and sporting events for the children, even after the home closed and right up to the dismantling of the camp around 1949. You name it; the kids saw it—even events near camp! He was a salesman who had vast contacts around the city and, unmarried, lived at the Ford Hotel in downtown Montreal.

His greatest joy was to see the smiling faces of the kids and to make them feel wanted and happy. He would visit often, usually at the evening meal, and distribute candy, treats, and ice cream for dessert. In appreciation for these treats, one of the older boys would get up and, in a loud voice, say, "Three cheers for Mr. Schalek, hip, hip, hooray, Tiger, hip, hip, hooray." The kids joined in, which always brought a smile to his face.

He was probably only in his late fifties or early sixties at that time. In the early 1950s, we learned sadly that he had passed away.

Mr. Sydney Levine, Staff and Board Member

Mr. Levine at the time was in his sixties or seventies, slim and full of energy. He was the dedicated camp handyman and carpenter for many years, along with the caretaker, Mr. Peter Tremp and family. He was a personal friend of Mr. Schalek.

One of his hobbies was to whittle little wooden miniature canoe paddles, very life-like, which he gave away to the kids who asked for souvenirs.

When he was seventy-two years old, the campers and staff organized a surprise birthday party for him, complete with a banner that read "Happy Birthday, Mr. Levine, 72 years young."

Mr. Levine was a great amateur carpenter and raconteur, and a real grandfather figure. The kids just loved him and loved to talk with him and learn from him. He spoke fluent French and was quite friendly with some of the local merchants in the village. His favourite expression was "What in the Sam Hill ...!"

Gerry Waldston, a camp counsellor whose sketches of camp kids and scenes Martin really enjoyed (two of these drawings are in Book One), would remember that Mr. Levine's greatest joy every year was to repair the wooden stairs that went down to the lake and up to the dining room—a very steep drop; he made them safe for the kids.

Recently, Martin Gordon gave Myer Gordon (no relation) the names of three of his buddies who were in the home—Billy Aaron, Oscar Muchnick, and Irving Levenson. Billy was thought to have been a watchmaker. They are all remembered by Annie Reisler Thomas because they were in her group. Martin, Billy, Oscar, and Irving had not been heard from since the homes closed, and the latter three are now deceased. Martin stressed that Billy had taken hundreds of photographs of the home and camp, and had hoped Myer could find them for the archives. Not likely, given that Billy is gone. But Martin is still actively pursuing the lost photos himself!

* * *

Myer Gordon

MONTEFIORE HOME

Since the first book, *Four Hundred Brothers and Sisters*, Myer remembers some more facts about his ten years in the Montefiore Home: the lack of toys generally, and he suddenly realized that he never had a real toy. The children improvised from household items they found *around*. They made a crystal radio from a second-hand set, attaching the tiny wires to the radiators; balls were socks stuffed with newspapers; fishing rods and bows and arrows emerged from old wire hangers and umbrellas.

Myer vaguely recalls being in the Wolf Cubs, wearing the green shirt and little cap. And a ritual that became a naughty joke many years later—"dip, dip, daub, daub, hands up to head ..." He also recalls losing his tonsils, and three days in the infirmary having his fill of ice cream and Jell-O!

"My mother called me Sonny at times—maybe she forgot my name! And when she came to visit me every few years, she'd ask, 'Did you miss me?' Me—'only when I'm not busy!'

Is that a commercial for an orphanage or not?!"

Myer's sunny attitude carries on even today. With his two artificial knees, he still talks about taking tap dancing lessons—the ones planned just before he realized he required knee surgery. He can't even walk half a block on pavement, but still dreams of tap dancing! But grass is good for golfing!

* * *

Shirley Israel Thau

MONTREAL HOME

That miserable, cold, rainy night in November 1935, my parents had been invited to the wedding of my father's favourite nephew (who also had been orphaned quite young). My mother had been suffering from a nasty cold and should not have gone out but she insisted on accompanying my father.

From what I can remember, my father brought my mother home early that night—her cold had gotten worse and she was quite ill. Soon after, she was taken by ambulance to the hospital, suffering from pneumonia. Sulpha drugs had only just been discovered and therefore were not in abundant supply.

Approximately two weeks later, my mother died. She was thirty-five! My parents had been married only eight years, and, needless to say, my father was a broken man. My brother Harvey was only seven years old; I was five and a half.

Since my family was not in any position to take on the care of two small children, my father thought it best to put us in the Montreal Hebrew Orphans' Home.

My brother went in early in 1936. I had contracted scarlet fever and chicken pox and went into Alexandria Hospital. Well again, I had to return to hospital to have my tonsils removed. It wasn't until the summer of 1936 that I entered the home. The staff and children were out in the country—Shawbridge, where their camp was situated. This camp had burned down in '22 after which a new camp was opened in Sainte-Marguerite-du-Lac-Masson, a really beautiful spot.

I can't really remember too much about my six years in the orphanage. Although we were taught many things, such as Hebrew, weaving, and elocution at the Dorothy Davis and Violet Walters School, and took part in Brownies and Girl Guides, I was not too thrilled with the place.

We had our own bus, with *MHOH* painted on the sides, which took us to school each day. None of the Westmount schools would or could accept over one hundred kids from an institution. Therefore, we had to travel down to Berthelet School, which was on Ontario Street at Bleury—quite some distance from the home. The Ladies' Benevolent Society (a Protestant orphanage, I thought) was right next door to the school, and when our bus arrived in the winter, a barrage of snowballs were hurled at us. That was the extent of violence in those days—nothing too serious and mostly in fun.

I remember becoming friends with a girl in school—Camille Weber. One day after school I was invited home with her. Without giving it much thought, I went. Naturally, I missed the MHOH bus and since I didn't have any money to take the city bus, I walked from McGill College and Burnside (now de Maisonneuve) back to the home on Claremont. I suppose I was punished for doing this and probably was sent to bed without any supper, but I didn't care. I had spent a lovely afternoon with someone outside the home.

The best times were Sundays, when my father came to visit (until he died in 1940 at age fifty-two). I was never allowed to keep any of the pretty clothes or toys he had purchased for me since it wouldn't have been fair to the other kids. I understand that now, but didn't then. After my father passed away, his brother, my Uncle Isadore, a bachelor, undertook our guardianship (for me and my brother Harvey), and visited us each Sunday. We usually went to an aunt's house to visit.

We used to have to go to bed quite early, when it was still light out. One evening, I could not fall asleep and began to hum softly to myself. Our dorm contained six to eight girls, and one of them found my humming annoying and warned me that if I didn't stop, she would report me to the girls' supervisor. I was defiant and would not bow down to this girl's threats, and continued to hum. Sure enough, the supervisor came and said if I didn't stop at once, she would take drastic steps. By this, she meant bringing in the boys' supervisor. Still I didn't stop, and when the boys' supervisor arrived, he proceeded to give me the thrashing of my life. The head of the home heard the commotion and came up to our floor and put a stop to it. I ended up with a swollen lip and bruises. I think I was about ten at the time.

Another happy time—Sunshine Camp in Sainte-Marguerite. They accepted many city kids, which enabled us to meet new kids. I am still friends with one such girl.

There was a very kind man, Arthur Schalak, who used to get passes for us to attend quite a few events, such as the Circus, the Ice Capades, the Ice Follies, bicycle races, and movies. He was also connected with bottling companies and we were often treated to soft drinks, which was a rarity.

I even recall misbehaving around Christmas. As punishment, I was put into isolation and sent off to the home's hospital on the top floor of the building. The nurse was a Mde. Clarke, who had a Christmas tree and always let me hang my stocking, and in the morning, I always found little treats or gifts. I loved being isolated at Christmas!

When I was about twelve, the powers-that-be felt I was a problem child, and asked my uncle to find another place for me to live. I went to live with an aunt. I wasn't much happier with her; she had only had boys and was not used to handling the care of a girl. It wasn't until just before her death that she mellowed and showed a soft side to her nature.

Perhaps it's because I'm an independent spirit and would rather have been raised normally by my own parents that I hated being in the orphanage. From 1942 until I graduated from high school in 1947, I looked forward to the day when I would be on my own. The orphanage closed about six months after I had been released, and the kids who were left were placed either with relatives or put in foster homes—my brother Harvey was put in a foster home.

I suppose life could have been a lot worse, in fact, I'm sure of this. But to be perfectly honest, I would have much preferred that my parents lived a long life and that I remained in their care.

I've forgotten many episodes—that's just as well. One remembers happy times, and I was just biding my time until the day I was on my own. I probably have made several mistakes in my lifetime, but all in all, I would say that I have been a pretty contented person and have always made my own way.

* * *

Willie Label

MONTEFIORE HOME

My father passed away when I was two or three years old, in 1922. By age four, my Mom had placed me in the Montefiore Orphans' Home. I remember my mother and me being in the office with Mr. Talpis, the office manager. I was pulling on my mother's skirt, crying my eyes out. She picked me up, placed me on the large steel safe, and a few moments later, she left. I remember kicking the safe and sobbing for a long time after she left.

I enjoyed the home very much once I got used to it, but there are only a few things I remember. I remember one of the kids was Sam Zitser, who was in my class, and one day Sam did not come to school and the teacher asked me how Sam was and I said he was fine. The next day Sam passed away; I guess I didn't know how sick he was.

> An unveiling today at 11 a.m., Sunday, September 18, 1927, at the B'nai Jacob Cemetery, Back River, for Samuel Zitser, late of the Montefiore Orphans' Home.
> Rabbi Vachtfogel will officiate.
> *Submitted by Eiran Harris*

Life in the home was not always fun and games. All the realities of life had to be faced, including death. Death was the dark side, especially when it involved the children.

I hated kasha; I used to make *parcels*—wrapping the kasha into napkins—and throw it down the drain (much like Benny Garber and his porridge parcels). I love kasha now!

I remember Wednesday was fish day—I loved fish and still do. Saturdays we were served half an orange and one egg, and we got lots of farina and porridge for breakfast, and cocoa with the skin on top—we called it by the Jewish word, *hoit*.

My buddy Abe Senderoff joined me as we *very* often went down to the back door in the early morning, opened the big steel cans of milk, and chewed the cream.

We also managed to slip into one of the pantries in the basement—we loved the homemade strudel there! Several of us took the strudel with us when we went to Fletcher's Field (now Mount Royal Park) and sat on the benches and just pigged out. Of course we were caught, but that's another story. (Watch for *Crime and Punishment*, Vol 2.)

I went to Baron Byng High School for four years and remember at recess I would go to the hot-dog stand and smell the hot dogs, I couldn't afford to buy one.

It seems that most of my memories are of food!

After I had been in the home for about eight years, Gisella Friedman arrived. She was studying to become a doctor. Abe and I played tennis with her on a neglected, burned-out tennis court on a beautiful lake during the summer months.

Sometimes my mother came and took me to visit some of her friends. I loved to go to one friend's house because her son had a tricycle, and I was able to ride it a little—what a treat!

I also remember there was a radio up on a ledge in the basement dining room. Saturday afternoons we would listen to *Live from the Metropolitan Opera*. Sometimes Giselle would join us. That's when I developed a taste for classical music.

When I left the home in 1935, I rented a room with my alumni buddy, Abe Senderoff. I then went back to live with my dear mother and found work in a carpet store, United Imports and Jobbers, in the Balfour Building, corner Saint-Laurent and Prince Arthur—but not for long. The carpets were too heavy! I wasn't by any means a big guy, and the carpets weighed more than I did! So I went to work in the ladies' wear trade until I joined the Air Force. When I returned, I got a good job with the government, overseeing the wages and work conditions of the labour force.

I can truly say that my years in the orphanage helped in my life as it is today. I think my obsession with food was one reason I am so healthy today. At eighty-three, I swim and play tennis nearly every day while wintering in Florida. And I am fortunate to have great children and grandchildren to add to my enjoyment of life.

* * *

Jack Miller

MONTREAL HOME

I was three months old in 1933 when my mother was sent to the Douglas Hospital. She was diagnosed, as we later discovered, with postpartum depression, and spent the rest of her days at the hospital. My father, Azreal Miller, was left with four children, Morris, aged thirteen; Loretta, also known as "Yetta," eleven; Eli, seven; and me.

Eli and Loretta entered the Claremont home at the time of mother's illness, around 1933–34, and I arrived in 1938 at the age of five to join my brother Eli, by then eleven or twelve and a well-liked resident. At the time of my arrival, Loretta was sufficiently mature to leave Claremont and went to live in a foster home. Morris was old enough to remain with my dad.

I vividly recall entering the home on that dramatic first day. I had been crying on the streetcar all the way there, and remember sitting in a park across the street and begging my kind foster mother, Mrs. Mayer, not to make me enter. But soon I had a wonderful experience in store in the form of my brother Eli, with whom, for the first time, I became very close.

I can't remember very much about my first years, but one thing that sticks is being scolded by a Mr. Ogulnick, an administrator. He made me stand at attention in front of him. I can't remember whether he hit me or not, but I do recall crying and having to repeat many times over, "I'm sorry, I didn't mean it, and I won't do it anymore."

A special day always was Sunday—visiting day. My father was a candy manufacturer who would bring boxes of many delights for all the kids: peanut brittle, sugar peanuts, hard candies, and Passover candies, to mention a few! Eli, known as "Shaver," and by now a potentate, was in charge of distributing the goodies, which, as it happens, took all week long.

Weekdays we were all taken by bus to Berthelet School. As this was in many ways the most formative period of learning, it is too bad that we were left on our own to figure out how to study. It took me years to discover how much I had missed not having a mother and father and a home environment to guide me.

We all looked forward to the summer and our two months at Sunshine Camp. This was a happy time for all, because we got to play games like baseball and basketball. We also went swimming and boating (with Eli serving as a life guard). It was great while it lasted, but then it was back to the Claremont home and the start of a new school year.

Certainly I made some good friends at the home, among them, Sammy Schwartz, Oscar Mutchnick, and Jacky Schneider (who was to tutor me in high school). I also learned how to skate and play hockey, because the rink was right in the backyard. In fact, we used to sneak out of the yard by climbing the fence and proceed down the hill to the candy store on Sherbrooke Street. And yes, we were sometimes caught and punished!

At age ten, I was taken out of the home and went to live with my dear Auntie Channa and Uncle Benny Tooberman. I didn't know what to expect, but was very much looking forward to a life with fewer barriers.

Over the years, I've stayed in Montreal and have held various administrative posts with several clothing manufacturers. I married my wife, Janice, in 1961 and we are still together. My daughter Vicki came along in 1970 and son Andrew in 1972. Grandkids include Sir and Naxa.

* * *

Aaron Palmer

MONTREAL HOME

Excerpted from an article by Lucille Groll, which appeared in a circular of the Beth Israel Synagogue, Kingston, Ontario, in 2003.

Aaron was born in Toronto in 1917, the only son of Solomon and Sarah Palmer. Solomon and Sarah were married in Kingston, Ontario, before moving to Toronto where their stay was very short, because they soon moved to Montreal.

When Aaron was eight years old, his father died. To add to the tragedy, his mother became ill and was hospitalized at a sanatorium in Sainte-Agathe. Unable to care for her young son, she regretfully had him accepted at the Montreal Hebrew Orphan's Home, where he lived until he was sixteen years old. Aaron still talks fondly of his mother, describing her as a very gentle, intelligent woman, highly regarded by all.

Aaron's experiences at the orphanage were positive, and he has pleasant memories of those years. Mr. Rosen was the superintendent; Max Matt his assistant. Some of his friends in the home were Abie Dubin, Henry and Joe Fox, Bert Scotcoff, Jack Raven, and George Sobel—Max's best friend. Aaron also remembers Max's sister, Hilda.

The home housed about one hundred children, and although in the Westmount area, Aaron remembers not being allowed to attend the local primary school; he had to go into the city centre by streetcar. On school days, all the children from the orphanage went to the Baron de Hirsch building on Bleury and Ontario (now Maisonneuve) for lunch. His mother and family visited him regularly. Summers were spent at Shawbridge Summer Camp.

Bar mitzvahs were held as group events with each boy having a very small part of the service. When the boys became of age to leave the orphanage, each one was told that, at the time of their bar mitzvah, a small amount of money (from benefactors) had been set aside for them that they were entitled to use on leaving. Aaron recalls that he refused this money; he knew he did not need it and could work.

This characteristic still describes Aaron, who is independent and self-sufficient; he appreciates all he has. When he was sixteen, he graduated from Commercial High School and, shortly after being discharged from the home (the Byes were then matron and supervisor), moved with his mother to Kingston. Both his parents had brothers in Kingston (Benjamin Palmer and Louis Routbard), so Aaron's connection to the Kingston Jewish community started long before he was born.

In 1934, Mrs. Palmer and Aaron had $500 that they used to open a small corner grocery store on the corner of Markland and Patrick streets. Aaron laughs as he remembers that the wholesaler lent them a scale! Financially, it was a very difficult time, and 50 per cent of customers bought on credit, often unable to pay the full amount owing at the end of the month. In a very typical Aaron attitude, he exclaims, "What could you do?" The store did well, but was sold in 1941 when Aaron went to France, Belgium, and Holland with the 4th Armored Division as a sergeant. In 1946, he was the very proud recipient of a Commander in Chief certificate, signed by General Montgomery, for outstanding service and great devotion while on duty during the campaign in northwest Europe.

When he returned from Europe, he worked for a short while with Veterans Affairs, and then bought a small business at the corner of Bay and Montreal streets. He remained there for five years, and, after trying other ventures, he opened Palmer's Grill in 1955; it became a well-known Kingston landmark, owned by Aaron until 1965. He also invested in other properties including a laundromat, which has become a gathering place for Queen's University students.

Though he always worked very long hours and often had little time for many other activities, Aaron and his mother were very much part of the Jewish community. He belonged to B'nai Brith and went to shul for Yartzeits and Jewish holidays.

Everyone who knows Aaron is aware that his great love is fishing, and he continues to enjoy this activity summer and winter. Norma, whom he married in 1970, used to also enjoy fishing, but now is happy to let Aaron go alone or with friends—every morning he meets a group of friends for coffee. But he and Norma share many interests and both keep active.

Since his retirement from Palmer's Grill, Aaron has become very involved in his synagogue; he spent many years on the Beth Israel Board, at one time holding the position of vice-chairman, and was involved in many major renovations at both the synagogue and the rabbi's home. He is also an ardent supporter of Israel.

Aaron is now eighty-seven years old. His quiet, efficient, and non-attention-seeking personality is still very evident on a daily basis to those who know him. Few know all the daily contributions he makes to enrich the individual lives of some of the collective needs of others. This is Aaron's way!

And, he is very happy to be reunited, in memories, through *Four Hundred Brothers and Sisters*. He wrote about a recent conversation with his old supervisor, Max Matt, that he found him to be "pretty chipper, considering he must be well into his nineties." Actually, Max will be ninety-four on Christmas Day, 2004!

* * *

Annie Rosenbaum (Gert Rose) Gordon

MONTREAL HOME

Submitted by her son, Sheldon Gordon, New York

My mother, born Annie Rosenbaum, and her two brothers, Hyman and Sydney, all were at the Claremont orphanage for various lengths of time after their mother died. My mother was in the first group to be admitted to the home in 1921, and her brothers apparently were admitted very soon thereafter. Unfortunately, none of them spoke much about their experiences at the time, so the family today has little information to provide about them at this time.

My mother eventually left the orphanage to live with her aunt and uncle. At the time, she changed her surname legally to Rose and also dropped her given name, Annie, and used her middle name, Gertrude, or simply Gert. So for the rest of her life, she was Gert Rose, and then, after getting married, Gert Gordon. Hyman took the English name Herbert, though he was known as Herbie Rose to everyone. Sydney was known as Sid Rose. I suspect that, because of the name changes, my mother and her brothers got lost in the history of the two orphanages.

As soon as she was able to, my mother got a job working at a jeweller's in downtown Montreal and immediately rented her own room with a family on Jeanne-Mance. She then assumed responsibility for Herbie and Sid, whom she brought out of the orphanage to live with her. She also had a younger sister, Sylvia, who initially stayed with their father, who did not particularly treat her, nor the other children, well. Sylvia was eventually removed from her father's care and taken in by a caring family who raised her.

My mother remained in Montreal until around 1938, when she came to New York to attend a wedding. It was there that she met my father, Hyman Gordon, and they were soon married. She spent the rest of her life in New York, originally working in my father's family store, a delicatessen that his father had opened when he came to these shores. They closed the store in 1956, and my mother began working as a secretary at a number of major firms, where she eventually worked her way up to some fairly responsible positions, including the head cashier at the Monsanto Corporation headquarters in the Empire State Building. She raised her two sons by herself after my father's death in 1958.

Clearly though, the upbringing she had at the Montreal orphanage and the schools in Montreal stood her in outstanding stead—she was well read, could write unbelievably well, and had an incredibly high work ethic. Throughout her life, she was totally dedicated to my brother Steve and to me, as well as to our wives and children. She passed away just days short of her ninetieth birthday.

Unfortunately, as I said above, she spoke relatively little about her childhood in Montreal, though one story she continually recounted was being the star pitcher on the Baron Byng baseball team. It probably was a good connection that she eventually lived fairly close to Yankee Stadium in the Bronx. Another story that she often recounted was the second place prize she won at the Jewish Endeavour Sewing School, Baron de Hirsch Institute for Sewing. Her prize was a siddur—a treasured keepsake which she gave to her only granddaughter.

My uncle Herbie remained in Montreal, married, and had one daughter, Sheilah. He became a very successful businessman, starting a number of companies throughout his life. He was very active in the Knights of Pythias and was very charitable, particularly toward Jewish causes, all his life.

My uncle Sid left Montreal and moved to the West Coast. He married and had two daughters, Sandee and Stephanie. He was very successful in the real estate business and very prominent in the social life of southern California.

The only remaining member of that generation is my aunt Sylvia, who moved to New York in 1949, and who still lives in the suburbs on Long Island. One of the stories she tells is of the time my mother brought her, as a very young child, to visit the orphanage and introduced her to my mom's many friends and the adults who kept the place going. In particular, my aunt recalls my mother introducing her to Mr. Irving Gerdy (superintendent, Montreal Home), and pleading with him to take her in also (probably to get my aunt away from their father). She promised to take good care of her little sister, but was turned down because Sylvia was too young at the time to be admitted.

While neither my brother nor I have much information about what happened to either our mother or her brothers at the orphanage, we can only surmise from their subsequent lives how much the orphanage did for them. They all grew up into successful individuals who were dedicated to their families and to Judaism.

That was a remarkable achievement and, as I see the stories of other graduates of the orphanages, it is evident that all of the children were similarly blessed.

* * *

Aaron Soloman (Abie Schmoiser)

MONTREAL HOME

Placed into the Westmount home at two years old (1931) ... not knowing the circumstances why, or who took care of me the first two years. To me, those in the home were my family. I attended Berthelet and Bancroft Schools and have wonderful, fond memories of Sunshine Camp, first in Shawbridge, then in the Laurentian Mountains. Mrs. Kammer [author thinks he means Mrs. Kramer], kitchen supervisor, was like a mother to me, always giving me extras to eat.

The home was very good to me, *except* for one physical beating that put me in the infirmary for two full weeks. I told one of the kids that Mr. Ogulnick (supervisor) was a drunk. Not knowing what it really meant, the kid went to squeal on me. I was put into the shower and strap beaten by Mr Ogulnick. Something that is very vivid 'til today. Was also friends with Abie Bye, whose father was president at that time. [Mr.Bye was a supervisor.]

We would always play sports with all the kids in the home, among them, Billy Aaron (the *pet* to Mr. Bye), Harvey Israel, and Eli Miller. Eli Miller's dad owned a candy store and he always brought me candies.

Sunday was visiting day. I never had visitors, unless Mr Schalek or Mr. Levine came. Does anyone remember Mr. Schalek (who also came to our wedding) or Mr. Levine? These men bring fond memories to me because they took us to the circus and to movies. They were like mentors, sort of the father and grandfather I did not have. Harvey Israel and I shared the same day and time of our bar mitzvahs. I also remember the name Moe Letnick and the Schwartz family—Sam, Harry, Leo, and Libby.

Shortly after my being bar mitzvahed, the home broke up. I was put into a foster home—Mr. and Mrs Engleberg, 4646 Esplanade. Not happy there. After eight months I left.

Joe and Morris Miller's mother, who lived at 5148 Saint-Urbain Street, offered me a room. To pay for this, I worked with Carl Wagner, who was doing the bread and cake transport delivery for Richstone Bakery. That's where I met Hymie Kogan, manager of Richstone's Bakery; he later left to go to Moishe's Steak House as manager.

Thereafter, at seventeen years, I met Dorothy, and history was made and my life changed. On January 1, 2004, we celebrated fifty-five years of marriage, and I was seventy-five on January 11. I'm still working in sales part time and living in Florida.

I look back with gratefulness to have been in the home. Today, I consider myself content with life and proud of my family—my wife, my children, and my grandchildren. Have travelled a lot and been blessed with pretty good health. Must agree, except for the traumatic loss of our first son at four years of age, the rest has been a blessing.

P.S. Billy Aaron was an usher at our wedding fifty-four years ago. We kept on being friends until we moved to Florida. He had moved from Montreal to Victoria, British Columbia. His trade was a watch repairer. Once he left Montreal, we did not hear from him. In 1995, when we flew to Vancouver to take an Alaskan cruise, upon our return we visited Victoria and looked for him by checking telephone books, jewellery shops, and inquiring about watchmakers around town. We could not locate him and have always wondered what happened to him. Should you find out we would appreciate learning what you know.

Met Jack Zukerman this morning. My gosh! So many years have passed. Says he recognized me, except for now being all grey. Well, we're both up there and grey—we all are. Had a delightful breakfast and reunion. He keeps quite busy. We talked and talked catching up on our lives. Brought some photos of my family and needless to say, he agreed with me that I hit lucky with my good-looking and loving family.

It was a very warm feeling to see a lanceman, so to speak. A lot of water under the bridge for all of us over so many years. He too said he could have kicked that Ogulnick s.o.b.

Thanks, Myer, for getting us together. Keep in touch, and to Judy, our regards too.

* * *

Vita Shein Seidler

MONTEFIORE HOME

Vita was born in Russia. Soon after her birth, her mother died of typhus—then the scourge of Russia, and Europe in general—leaving Vita, her sister, and two brothers. Her father remarried and soon after had a son, Abie.

Father wanted to emigrate with his family to Canada, but the borders were closed to young children. So Vita and her brothers were *aged*—Vita from five to seven, Louis from fifteen to seventeen—to show he was old enough to take care of Vita and Abie. One brother and sister remained in Russia because they were the *wrong* age. Their stepmother remained with them—she couldn't speak English—and a single parent could take out only the number of children he or she could care for. After arriving in Montreal, Louis reverted to his real age; Vita kept her *new* age on her citizenship papers; her name was spelled Vitia—the way it was then pronounced.

Most of the family lived on Clark Street with cousins, seven people in a two-bedroom house. Louis boarded with another family. After one year, father, in his early thirties, had to go back to work but had no one to look after his children. So Vita and her half-brother, Abie, entered the Montefiore Home.

Vita liked being in the home with so many children who became her friends. She couldn't speak English at the beginning, and she so adored the matron, Mrs. Rachel, who not only spoke to her in fluent Russian but also gave her her first toy, a plastic doll, to make her feel more at home. Some of the other girls had dolls they made from rags.

Vita knew that her doll needed a place to sleep. She found a cardboard shoebox and lined it with a towel. To pull it like a carriage, she found two empty wooden spools from a sewing box, put a cord through each one, made holes in the shoebox and pulled the cord through. Very innovative for a five-year-old. Or was she seven?

She also knew enough to pierce a hole in its mouth so, when *feeding* it, the doll looked like it was peeing. That gave her a chance to play mother and change its wet bed!

Other girls followed her idea and they had many hours of play in the basement or in the dormitory near their beds. They knew enough not to bring the *carriage* outside because the cardboard might tear as they pulled it along for the dolls daily walk, acting like an adult with her child.

Vita entered kindergarten at Bancroft School. Kindergarten in those days was called *Scribble and Pencil*. She started learning English and, after only a few weeks, knew enough to get along with the other children.

Vita loved the home's supervisor, Max Matt. She couldn't wait for her birthday, because on that special day, Max would sit next to the celebrant at dinner. She felt so important. Her father ran the Passover Seders in the home while his children lived there. Vita was very proud of her father for doing this mitzvah.

Her stepmother came to Montreal four years later. One day she appeared at the home, told Vita and Abie she was their mother, and took them home. Vita, now nine, thought this was her real mother; she had no memory of her real mother, having spent those early years in Russia with her grandparents.

Vita continued school at Bancroft and recently came into possession of her report cards from those years. They caused some confusion because she was listed as being in kindergarten in 1928, and she had thought she only came to Canada in 1930 or 1931. As she became more proficient in English, her marks went from an F up to 81 out of 125, her spelling to 90. According to her report card, she seems to have skipped grade 4. Her report card also indicated one year with many days absent. Vita recalls she spent many months in the sanatorium with asthma-like symptoms. She remembers being so excited when Max Matt paid her several visits.

Now she really doesn't know how old she is! She finished public school and two years of high school, which she had to leave because her parents could not afford the $3 a month fee.

Her first job was in a factory, aged fourteen, folding curtains at $3 a week. And when she saved enough money, she went back to commercial high school, which enabled her to get an office job. Meanwhile, she had kept in touch with some of her friends from the home, Ida Sklar Lewis, Celia Wiseman (later Tina Rosen), and Mary Sokoloff, with whom she loved to travel. Her greatest love even today, aside from her family, is travelling.

One of her office jobs paid very well, $15 a week, but she was bored because there was not enough to do. Her boss really liked her, and before she left, fixed her up with Eric, who boarded with his family. Seven months later, Vita became Mrs. Eric Seidler, after a very, very small wedding.

She had been working at another small office with friend Mary, typing and doing general work. After marriage, she stopped working because she wanted to start a family right away. They had two sons, Norman and Barry, and Vita went back to work once they were in school. Her work, this time, was most satisfying—she stayed twenty-eight years, helping to run a printing business owned by a blind gentleman. While working, she went to McGill University at night for three years, taking psychology, but found it too much to look after her family, work, and go to school.

Vita and Eric moved to Toronto in 1990 to be near their sons and two grandchildren.

Brother Jack became a fighter pilot in World War II. After the war, he opened a clothing manufacturing plant and was very close to Vita's sons. Barry wanted to be just like his uncle Abie (who changed his name to Jack as an adult) and today owns his own clothing manufacturing company. Norman joined Pitney Bowes after graduating university and is now a travel agent.

* * *

Ida Sklar Lewis

Montefiore Home

In the last two years, I have suffered the loss of my two siblings. My sister, Yetta, who is the youngest of the three of us, passed first. Last March, my brother, Solly, passed away as well. I am the sole survivor of my immediate family. After much cajoling by my family and friends to write my biography, I am sitting at my kitchen table, trying to decide where to start. I guess the best place to start is at the beginning.

My parents and my brother, Saul (Solly), left Russia after the Revolution. They crossed the border illegally into Romania. Upon arrival in Bucharest, they found that both North and South America had closed their borders to new immigrants. My family was forced to settle down in Bucharest and wait for the next chance to immigrate to the New World.

I was born during this period of uncertainty. After many months, Argentina opened its doors to immigrants. My mother's brother, his family, and my parents were all prepared to leave the country and head to Argentina. Just before the ship set sail, my brother, Solly, became sick. They did not allow any sick people to get on the boat, so my family was forced to stay in Romania. My uncle left for Argentina, telling us that we should make the next crossing and meet him in South America. The next week, lo and behold, Canada opened its doors to immigrants. We took the ship and landed in Canada, eventually settling in Montreal.

I try to think of how hard it must have been for my parents to come to the New World on their own with two young children. You will have to bear with me, because there is no one to help me to recollect my memories. I remember that my mother grew ill. After she gave birth to my sister, Yetta, her health deteriorated. She endured fifteen surgeries over the next few years. I remember that children were not allowed to visit at the Royal Victoria Hospital, where my mother was staying. Instead, I remember that Solly, Yetta, and I stood up the hill on University Avenue and waved to my mother. She watched us out of her hospital room window and waved back. That was the last time that we saw her. She succumbed on November 11, 1931, at the age of thirty-two.

According to family and friends, my mother was a very beautiful woman, with a magnificent singing voice. Solly always told me about how she would sing to him from her hospital room window.

I must digress to tell you about Mrs. Mitnick, the cook at the orphanage. When I arrived at the home, she asked me my last name. Upon hearing that it was Sklar, Mrs. Mitnick further asked me if my mother's first name was Chana. I replied, "Yes." She told me that she was in the hospital the same time as my mother. The cook explained to me how, no matter how gravely ill my mom was, she always sang for the patients. Mrs. Mitnick further stated that she had never met anyone as nice as my mother. That made me proud to be her daughter.

After my mother passed away, my papa found himself incapable of emotionally and financially caring for all of us. Yetta and I were placed in the orphanage, while Solly stayed home with our father. The orphanage opened my eyes to new experiences and novel learning opportunities. It also provided us with a safe and nurturing environment. For the first time in my life, I felt as though someone was looking after me.

At home, my father always read the Yiddish news, and we never discussed the news with him. In the home, Mr. Matt read the *Montreal Star* out loud every night to us after supper and discussed the current events. That fuelled my interest in reading and exploring the world around me.

My years in the Montefiore Hebrew Orphans' Home were happy ones. I enjoyed being with friends who had been through similar traumatic experiences. We had great times together. Every weekend we participated in exciting activities. We went skating and tobogganing on Mount Royal and we often went to the movies. In other words, we had the opportunity to do all the same things as other children.

I remember the time when Mary Sokoloff convinced me to cut school to go to the movies. We attended Commercial High School on Sherbrooke and Saint-Urbain at the time. We carried our lunch bags to Saint-Lawrence and Duluth, waiting for the doors of the theatre to open for the day. All of a sudden, the worst thing that could ever happen happened! We caught sight of Mrs. Taube, our matron, approaching us. I thought I was going to die, but Mary was full of moxie, and she walked over and greeted Mrs. Taube. She quickly invented a story about how we were released from school to have our eyes examined at the optometrist nearby. Mary said that we would return to school after our examination, and Mrs. Taube said, "Fine," bid us to take care, and walked away. Needless to say, I was unable to enjoy the movie. I was afraid that Mrs. Taube would tell Mr. Matt. Boy, would we get it if he found out that we had cut school to go to the movies! Thankfully, she never said anything to us. That was the first and last time that I ever cut class!

I just wanted to relate a few things about my time at the MHOH. When the time came to leave the home, a whole group of us girls stuck together. Mary Sokoloff (of blessed memory), Vita Shein, Mamie Cohen, Tillie Hoffman, Tina Wiseman, and I never felt the need to make new friends, since we were the most comfortable with each other, like sisters.

After I left school, I went to work as a bookkeeper. I kept two sets of books—oy vey, if my boss only knew! I kept one set of books for my work in the office, and one set that I brought home nightly for my papa to check. Then, in 1941, my good friend, Gilda Lewis, insisted on setting me up with her older brother, Israel. "He's tall, dark, and handsome," she told me. "He has a widow's peak and looks just like Robert Taylor." I quickly agreed to meet him. Israel, who was shy, was dragged to my door by his two brothers. They rang the doorbell and ran, leaving Israel to greet me on his own. He was not any Robert Taylor, but he was a kind and gentle man. One year later, on June 20, 1942, we got married. Our marriage was a long and happy one, based on the love and friendship that we had for each other. Together we raised two wonderful daughters, Neile and Marlene.

During the Second World War, I started a Victory Club with some of my friends. We held parties, fashion shows, and races, for which we would charge admission fees. The money that we collected from the fees was donated to children whose fathers were fighting in the war. When the war was over, we started a chapter of the Heart Foundation in the name of my mother, Chana Sklar, and Bluma Silver, my friend Anne's mother. We worked doggedly to raise money that was desperately needed. We organized most of our events to coincide with the American Heart Foundation's events in February, so as to get free advertising! After many years, our chapter of the Heart Foundation became independent, and I moved on.

Next, I joined the Montreal Hadassah–WIZO, the Women's International Zionist Organization. I eventually became a member of the Executive Board, and chaired all of our undertakings, including the Bazaar, Israel Bonds, and Youth Aliyah. During my first mission to Israel, I met some of the children that we were looking after. These children had been brought to Israel from Ethiopia, Russia, and some of the countries from the Middle East. What a thrill it was to see their faces so bright and happy! Seeing the fruit of our labour made us all want to go home and start working all over again. In this way, I felt that my work with Hadassah–WIZO had enabled me to give back a little of the happiness and good memories that were given to me through my stay at the Montefiore Home.

In March, 1996, I lost my dearest friend. Israel was gone, and a new way of life began. My children and grandchildren, God bless them, looked after all of my needs as if I were a newborn babe. I wish for everyone's children to look after their parents as mine do.

My granddaughter, Stacey, was married in October, 1999. My grandson, Ilan, walked me down the aisle. It was a happy time, mixed with a little pathos. Time passed, and everything went along nicely. Candace, my younger granddaughter, passed her master's degree and is now in the fourth year of her PhD. This is what I call *naches*.

The happy times tasted bittersweet, as we watched Ilan's health deteriorate due to cystic fibrosis. He had had a successful double lung transplant, which allowed him to live several years in relatively good health. During that time, he tried to live out his dreams, doing everything that he had not been able to do before the transplant. He lived those post-transplant years to the fullest. Then, Ilan suffered from his body's rejection of his new lungs, and related infections. He was very ill, and we lost our dear Ilan.

Losing Israel was bad, but losing Ilan was worse.

Life has a funny way of sending you to the depths of hell and making you soar through the skies in delight. I say this, because shortly after Ilan passed away, Stacey gave birth to a beautiful little girl. She was named Ilana, B. H. after her cousin, Ilan. To us, Ilan is reborn. Ilana is wild about her auntie and uncle, and they are crazy about her. Need I tell you how I feel? Incidentally, I also have a new great-grandson, named Shane, and he truly is *shein*!

Now, I think I shall stop right here before this *bubbe's meinse* becomes a novel! That I will leave up to Judy Gordon, who is doing a great job.

* * *

Anita Wagon Bercovitch

MONTEFIORE HOME

My parents came from Russia around 1915. When I was six, my father passed away in 1923 after contacting TB—he was twenty-eight years old. My brother Sam and I stayed with my grandmother for a while, while my mother went to work at the Jewish Hospital. In 1926, she placed us in the Montefiore Home; Sam was four and a half, I was nine.

I enjoyed my years in the orphanage ... all the staff were very caring people. I loved the home, school, and summers in the country. My *kid* sister was Vita Shein. I remember Mrs. Milstein, the nurse, who treated us all very well—she had a wonderful sense of humour.

We left the home in 1930 when my mother remarried a Mr. Cherry, who had three of his own children in the same home—Rose, Dave, and Harry. I was thirteen. I remember when, in school in the same class as Dave, my teacher asked, "How come you and Dave have different names but the same address?" I answered, "Because my mother married his father!"

I did not go to high school because we couldn't afford the $3 a month.

Today, I appreciate the time I spent in the Montefiore Home; I am very proud of all it taught me. I now live in a seniors' residence. Nat and I have been married sixty-five years and have three great-grandchildren.

* * *

Gerry Waldston

MONTREAL SUNSHINE CAMP COUNSELLOR

December 6, 2003

Born in Berlin, Germany, on August 28, 1923, as Gerd Waldstein, to a typical German–Jewish line dating back to the sixteenth century, I was forced to leave my high school in the year of the Berlin Olympics. Due to my father's high rank during World War I, I had been allowed to stay until 1936 as the last Jewish student. My new, expensive Jewish school followed two parallel programs: the German curriculum, plus the British one with opportunities of matriculating in Cambridge. My education at age fourteen was equal to second year college in Canada.

We fled to England three months prior to World War II and established a factory in South Wales, which was destroyed by the first bomb that fell on British soil. When Dunkirk fell, no alien was allowed to live within twenty miles of the British coastline, which forced us to move into the mountains of South Wales.

In June 1939, my father and I were picked up as enemy aliens and placed behind barbed wire, together with some thousands of other males, in North Wales.

After one week, I was separated from my father and shipped across the ocean to Canada in a converted troop transport that also carried regular German POWs destined for the Canadian West. An earlier transport, the infamous *Arandora Star*, was torpedoed and sank, while British soldiers kept their Jewish prisoners at bay with fixed bayonets to keep them from the lifeboats. Only fifty Jewish captives survived.

After fifteen months behind barbed wire ... shunted from Monteith, Ontario, to Ripples Station, New Brunswick, and finally to Sherbrooke, Quebec, I was one of the first youngsters to be released (as a student) to a distant relative in Montreal, on probation. Without funds and no permit to work, I went to art schools during the day and worked at night to sustain myself, until my citizenship was granted in 1945.

In 1942 and again in 1943, I was hired as a counsellor at Sunshine Camp, together with my friends the late Joe Weininger* and Walter Odze.† We felt a rare kinship with these young boys and girls who came from broken and less fortunate homes. We understood what it meant to have little, to be an orphan and to fend for oneself in a selfish world. We tried to give these young people a taste of trust, teach them hygiene and good sportsmanship, and give them our full attention. It was also my introduction to Sainte-Marguerite, to which I returned year after year, winter and summer, as my second home. These formative years for all of us, as well as for our young charges, were among the happiest and most carefree times I can remember.

With no titles or full education, with only one talent under my belt, I climbed the ladder as a creative artist between 1945 and 1956, until I opened my own successful business, which is still in operation today, but run by my son Dan.

Today, at the venerable age of eighty, I can look back at the tumultuous years of have-not, days of hunger and the desire to succeed in my profession. With fluency in four languages plus four others for communication, I have a penchant for research in Mexican archaeology of over fifty years, and I am a collector of British stip-

* *Dr. Joseph Weininger—born in Vienna in 1923, brilliant scientist and one of the youngest PhDs at McGill, heading the electrochemistry department at G. E., Schenectady. Chairman of the American Chemical Society, lecturing in thirty countries prior to his early untimely death in 1990 at age sixty-seven. More than two dozen patents to his name. US Chess Champion in 1961, 1976, and 1987.*

† *Walter Odze—born in Hannover in 1923, one of the most brilliant designers in the electromagnetic field, as well as a superb pianist and exponent of Bach, an outstanding sportsman in tennis, golf, and skiing. President of a large manufacturing plant with over one hundred employees at the time of his untimely death in 1980. A rare human being with talents in so many fields—a tragic loss.*

ple engravings by Bartolozzi, and an ardent researcher of German philately and Canadian varieties; as well as a collector of anti-Semitic edicts from the middle ages to study the dissemination of hatred via the printed word.

[All the while] I am surrounded by my wonderful family—my wife, Shoshana, a Sabra and the highest ranking female officer in the 1948 War, and our three children and their delightful five consequences—truly the highest return in interest on my investment in love, learning, and our commitment to one another.

The orphanage on Claremount and the many threads that were spun from within these walls are very closely related to the many stories of success that grew from within the barbed wire—to the great benefit of our community and an ever-growing Canada.

Gerry Waldston continued ...

I have been wrestling with the material because, at my advanced stage of life—forgetting the names of these boys—there are only *slips* of memory. It's a tough job to make one's brain cells recall events of sixty years ago, yet some of these young boys from the home will forever be embedded in my mind.

There was Teddy Abrams—a bright young boy with a hoarse voice, who struck me as very exceptional. He articulated well and showed a great sense of humour, combined with a clean and frank attitude toward life, in spite of some obvious problems at home.

As it happens so often in life, I found myself working as an apprentice in the same firm as his father, a highly regarded graphic artist. I also met his two sisters, one of whom married someone in a circus. I heard that Teddy had been sent to the *Boys' Farm* in Shawbridge, from where he escaped and went home. He married, had a daughter, and joined the Merchant Navy. Haven't heard anything since—with great regrets because I felt that here was a very valuable person.

Another memorable lad, one of my young boys, was Martin Gordon, called *Brushy*, because he was always drawing at the home—a good, quiet lad who was swallowed up by the crowd. Never in trouble, never an oblique word.

Of course, there were the usual trouble-makers—young, exuberant boys with rebellious behaviour—whom I enjoyed the most because they showed spunk and character. I see them in front of me but cannot recall their names (I believe one was called Harry). One of them, I heard, had done very well and become wealthy, the aim of every young boy at Sunshine Camp. The other dream was to have bulging muscles.

I remember one incident where I had warned them of not playing the age-old, corny tricks on me, because I had experienced them over and over. That night, when I came into the hut, my bed and all my belongings had vanished into thin air. Great prank! I loved it! Of course, I knew the culprits—who were fast asleep. I took a long string and tied it around the big toes of each of the three ringleaders and woke *one* of them up! It created the proper answer and I was never bothered again ...

Then there was the Friday hike with my troupe of twenty. I knew the surrounding area like my pocket—the woods, the rivers, the swamps. We walked and marched and marched until I told them that we were lost! Made them climb up trees to find a road home, made them take off their clothes and shoes, carry them on their heads and walk and swim a fairly deep brook for about half a mile. Many a shoe and sock was lost, some of the boys could not swim and had to be *ferried* along. It was Shabbat night and we arrived bedraggled and ragged, but just in time to change into whites for dinner—there wasn't a sound to be heard that night from my bunks!

And I had a nicc heart-to-heart talk *on a carpet* for losing Federation clothes ...

There was Mrs. Kramer, a kindly lady who enjoyed her work, looking after the boys during mess time ... there was Dr. Gross, a fine young doctor who married a lovely young lady and went to Israel, where I visited him in his home.

As I am writing these spotty memories, a flood of faces appears before me, recollection of photos from long ago that are still embedded in my mind. The faces are real, the names are forgotten, but can be instantly evoked once I see them in print.

Thanks to the *Mishpocha* (the MHOH alumni newsletter), these names become meaningful every time I read them.

Myer, your excellent job of keeping the past alive and holding your *family* together is worthy of the highest award—the Order of Canada comes to mind!

* * *

Celia Wiseman (Tina Rosen)

MONTEFIORE HOME

Submitted by daughter, Connie Rosen, December 2003

My mother entered the Montefiore Hebrew Orphans' Home on Jeanne-Mance at the age of seven, just after her mother died. Her Yiddish name was Tsippa. My mother had an older sister named Celia who was not placed in the home and for some strange reason. Mr. Matt, the supervisor of the home, started calling my mother Celia, so everyone called her Celia until she left the home and changed her name to Tina (the English translation).

Although she spent only a year or two in the home, she always said that it was one of the happiest times of her life. The food was good and there was enough to go around. My mother told me that she loved the breakfasts—especially the porridge—so much so that she used to eat some of the other kids' porridge but *only* if they didn't want it!

There were other kids to play with, and everyone went to Bancroft School. Even the kids who lived in the neighbourhood came to visit. One of these neighbourhood kids happened to be my father—although they didn't meet until about seventeen years later.

Many lasting friendships were made amongst *the kids*. One in particular for Tina was with Vita Shein Seidler. Whenever there was an entertainment evening in the home, Tina and Vita used to get up to sing. One of their favourite songs was *I Sat Seven Years in the Prison*. (I'd like to get the words to that song!)

They used to sneak food at the end of the day just in case they did something wrong and were punished. One such incident occurred when they each took a tomato back to their room and they heard the matron coming. They hid their tomatoes under the covers on their beds and sure enough the matron came in and sat down on Vita's bed on the tomato!

When they had a masquerade night, Tina went dressed as Night and Day. She cut a hole in a sheet. One side was white and the other side was painted black. She put her head through the hole in the sheet and wore it with a sense of pride and fun!

The summer camp in the Laurentians was the best. There were all kinds of activities—swimming, outdoor games, sports. *The kids* were carefree and happy and got a lot of enjoyment just being away from the city and their regular routines. After Tina left the orphanage to live with her father and other siblings, she went back to Devonshire School, but often returned to the home to visit and play with her friends who were still in the home. In the summers, she always went back to the camp run by the MHOH.

In 1946, shortly after my father, Leonard Rosen, returned from overseas, they met and then married in March 1947. They were married for fifty-five years and had two beautiful children, a daughter, Connie (me), and then my brother, Howard. They also have three grandchildren—Elisa, Bianca, and Simon, whom they adore. I believe that because of Tina's experience in the home, both she and my father made our home a very happy one filled with love and affection.

My mom looked forward to every MHOH reunion; she and my dad attended all of them—whether in Montreal or Toronto. I attended one of the reunions in Toronto held at Myer and Judy's home on a Sunday afternoon in 1989. There were so many people, inside the house, outside on the lawn, I couldn't remember what name belonged to what face.

My mom died in October 2002, but my dad and I attended the reunion in September 2003; I am very glad we went. Through pictures and actually meeting some of *the kids*, I was finally able to put faces to the names of the people whom Tina had always spoken so lovingly about.

I want to thank Myer and Judy for their efforts in keeping the brothers and sisters in touch with each other through their newsletters and reunions, and for giving me the opportunity to write about my mom.

* * *

The Wyne Sisters

IN THE ORIGINAL MONTREAL HOME

By Soryl Shulman Rosenberg, Westmount, Quebec

The Wyne sisters were four in number. The oldest was Hilda. She was born in Manchester, England, in 1902 to Sarah Brodie and Julius "Jack" Wyne. Julius already had two sons named Wolf and Sam. By 1905, they had emigrated to Sherbrooke, Quebec, where Ida was born in that year. In 1907, Nancy was born, followed by Simmie in 1909.

In 1912, father Julius died, leaving four young daughters and a wife of thirty years of age, as well as his two teenage sons. Sarah, his widow, moved to Montreal where it was easier for her to get assistance from the Baron de Hirsch Institute.

In 1914, Sarah died from pneumonia at the age of thirty-two. Her daughters were placed in a home on Jeanne-Mance and then in the home at 500 Claremont. [I think the writer meant the original home on the corner of Evans and Cecil streets, which served as an orphanage, old folks, and sheltering home—for poor, newly arrived immigrants—the Jeanne-Mance home did not open until 1921.]

Hilda, the eldest, married Charles A. Benjamin in 1921 when she was nineteen. She married him with the understanding that her three sisters would move in with them. Because Hilda was a minor when she married, A. M. Vineberg and Charles Fisher acted as tutor and sub-tutor respectively on her behalf.

Charles Fisher was a Board member of the Montefiore Home ... he and his wife, Anna, used to visit the children all the time; he had a ladies' wear store on Guy Street at that time. Niece Soryl Rosenberg believes it was Charles Fisher who had introduced Charles Benjamin to Hilda. Hilda and Charlie became good friends with Charles and his wife, and their friendship lasted for many years.

Hilda and Charlie had two sons, Gerald and Peter. Gerald became president of *Benjamin News*. He married Patricia Pearson and they had three children Paul, John, and Jane. Peter became a pediatrician and lives in Houston with his wife, Sonia Grover—they also had two sons and one daughter, Eugene, Lloyd, and Louise. Hilda died in 1990.

Ida worked in Montreal as a legal secretary for Bras Campbell and also in New York. She married Aaron "Jimmy" Shulman (Shulman Cartage) in 1939 and had two children: a daughter Soryl who married Gilbert "Gibby" Rosenberg, and a son Gerald who lives in Israel. Ida died in 1997.

Nancy married Bruce Ogilvy and lived in Osoyoos, British Columbia, all her married life. She and Bruce had two sons, Robert and Blair. Robert "Bob" lives in Delta, British Columbia; Blair remained in Osoyoos. Nancy died in 1998.

Simmie, who never married, worked for *Benjamin News* and loved the horse races! She died, but the year of her death is unknown.

Charlie Benjamin remained connected to the home. A generous man to his family and a philanthropist to the community, his sons Gerald and Peter remember that in the early 1930s, he donated several rowing boats to the summer camp at Shawbridge.

* * *

Sylvia Zimmerman (Sherry Grossman)

MONTEFIORE HOME

Reminiscing—sixty years later (1934–1941). Not easy to do.

My dad died when I was five years old. My mother had no means of support, so she put me in the Montefiore Hebrew Orphans' Home. I was there for two years, after which we were all transferred to the MHOH in Westmount.

Skinny, straight blond hair, shy, and afraid, I was placed in a large dormitory with authoritarian large strangers. I am trying to recall counsellors, teachers, and friends.

Some were mean and cruel (I said a bad word and had my mouth washed out with soap; I can't imagine what I said). As time passed, I know that I made many friends—my peers were wonderful, yet I was teased a lot, for example: "Sylvia's hair is like the day, long and straight and looks like hay"—imagine, I still remember.

We ate in a large dining hall and were forced to finish everything, even if the food was awful. We also had to say prayers. Many a tear was shed. [Cheder] Hebrew classes were mandatory—my memories of these are not pleasant—the ruler across my knuckles still smarts.

My main memory is that for over nine years we lived without choices: We were given clothing to wear; we lived by bells—got up in the morning, ate with the bell, went to bed by the bell. Most activities were forced! No choices!

In retrospect, we learned many things: knitting, sewing, and weaving. We had dance classes, which we loved. I can still recall the "Grand March" from *Aida*, and dancing to the "Waltz of the Flowers" from the *Nutcracker Suite*, and learning many Gilbert and Sullivan songs.

The best day was Sunday! My mother brought goodies and we shared many wonderful hours. Wonderful happy memories of Mr. Schalek. That man was our Santa Claus. He arranged for us to attend all major attractions at the Forum. We saw hockey games, ice shows, and circuses. If any great event came to Montreal, he managed to get seats for the orphans from the home.

Summers were the best! Camp Sunshine, gold and blue ... swimming, hiking, boating, relay races, and young handsome counsellors (male and female volunteers). We picked blueberries and I can still taste the jam with ice-cold milk that we enjoyed overlooking Lake Marguerite.

I left the home either in 1940 or 1941. My mother took me to New York to live with her brother. She remarried in 1947 and moved to New Jersey. I graduated from junior college in 1948 ... I feel I had a good education, learned discipline, and am able to adjust and make friends easily. I love having choices!

I was at the UN when Israel was declared a country! I was there with a group of young people from Habonim, a labour Zionist organization. We were way up in the balcony, but it was very exciting—an important moment in history!

I married Ivan Grossman in 1951—he was a business man, very active in organizations. My expertise is art, and I chaired many successful art shows and sales (both in New Jersey and in California), raised funds for many Jewish organizations, Israel Bonds, UJA, National Council, Ort—you name it, I did it ...

In 1961, Ivan decided he wanted to work in the medical area, so he went back to college (my alma mater) and took the MCA—he must have killed it! He was accepted in five schools, and we chose Stanford, California (good weather, great golf country). Imagine, my poor mother passed away in 1961 and never knew her daughter married a doctor. Have three *gojus* daughters and three grandchildren, also *gojus*! My hobbies: bridge, poker, gin (love cards), and golf. We have travelled all over—Paris, Rome, England, the Soviet Union, Korea—really, very lucky. I also went on four missions to Israel.

Despite several physical problems the past couple of years, I am still active and having fun. I feel that I had a charmed life.

Sherry and Dr. Ivan Grossman now live in Los Altos, California but are moving near Sacramento by October 2004. She has attended several reunions in Montreal and keeps in touch with the Gordons.

* * *

A Guide for Perplexed Mothers

The Care of the Child

By

Alton Goldbloom, M.D.

This work originated through noting, over a period of years, the type of questions most frequently asked by young mothers, and by taking into consideration the points which worried them most concerning their children. An attempt has been made to give correct information on the development, care and feeding of the child.

Price $1.50

BURTON'S LIMITED

Booksellers and Stationers

1243 St. Catherine Street West,

Telephone Up. 3441 Near Mountain St.

1928

On the same page as the above ad were articles about a November Talmud Torah Bazaar, held on Brunswick Street, and a Hadassah Tea with guest Dr. Vera Weizmann, president of W.I.Z.O., and wife of Dr. Chaim Weizmann, president of the World Zionist Organization. Present was Mrs. A.J. Freiman of Ottawa, one of the founders of Hadassah and with sporadic connections to the Montreal orphanages.

Mrs. L. Miller was then president of the Montreal Chapter; Mrs. E. Lozinski "Rendered vocal solos with Mrs. M.N. Fineberg at the piano." Also present were Mesdames H. Abramowitz, E.G. Bernstein, M.H. Cohen, L.D. Crestohl, L. Fitch, F. Harris, L. Kline, S. Jaffe, A. Levin, H. Singer, J.L. Zlotnick.

This page and those following contain advertisements from the *Canadian Jewish Chronicle* of 1928, 1929, 1930.

Enjoy the memories, and it's okay to chuckle a bit, too!

The above ad is from 1928

TURKISH BATH

DOCTORS RECOMMEND
and
PHYSICAL CULTURE
Experts Always in Attendance
at the
DE LA SALLE TURKISH
BATHS
Single Baths and Massage, $1.25

10 Tickets for $10.00

Physical Culture Bath and
Massage
10 TICKETS FOR $15.00
Ladies daily from 10 a.m. to 5 p.m
Mondays 10 a.m. to 10 p.m.
Except Saturday and Sunday
Gentlemen daily, 5 p.m. to 10 a.m.
Sat. from 12 a.m. to Mon. 10 a.m.

De La Salle Turkish Bath

1334 DRUMMOND STREET

THIS TO THE LADIES!

As you do your Shopping,
Into all the stores a-popping,
Into street cars, changing, chopping,
Tired as you can be,
Horn's will find a restful stopping
Place for lunch or tea.

Special For Thursday

Corned Beef and Cabbage a la Dinty Moore. A real man's meal.

35c

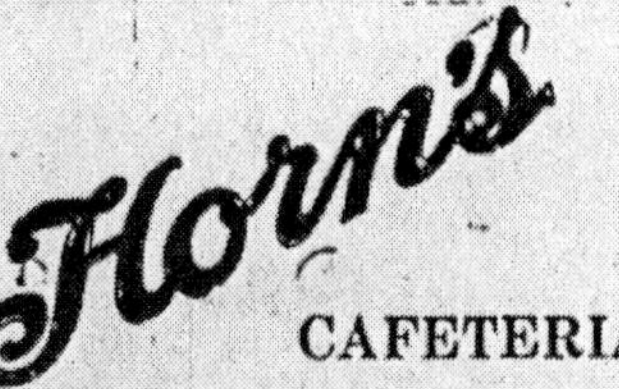

CAFETERIA

Bleury Street above
St. Catherine
(On the West Side)

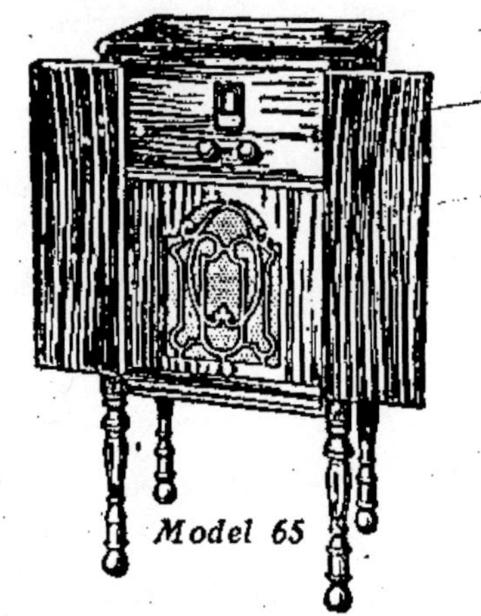

A rich walnut console houses the one-dial six tube Radio receiver built-in Speaker. Light socket operation. With tubes.

$232

Lyric *Mohawk* Radio

Electric Appliances Reg'd

641 St. James St., Montreal
Wholesale Distributors.
L. B. Bessette, Manager

Is your Radio sick?

We specialize in repairs for any make of set.

A Fully-equipped Service Car at Your Disposal.

Call Lan. 7259

ATLAS RADIO SALES

1408 MANSFIELD

Authorized Mohawk and Koltzer Dealer.

EASY TERMS ARRANGED

1928

HIS MAJESTY'S

MONTREAL'S LEADING THEATRE

Telephones UP. 9450-9644

NEXT WEEK - - - - SEATS NOW

THE LONDON PLAYERS Present

The Gay Unique and Fascinating Comedy Drama

"DEAR OLD ENGLAND"

A Whimsical Play by H. S. MALTBY

With EDWARD RIGBY and English Cast

Eves.: 50c to $2.50. Wed. Mat. 50c to $1.50. Sat. Mat. 50c to $2.

She Talks! IN THE SEASON'S MOST AMAZING COMEDY-DRAMA

LILLIAN GISH

— IN —

"ONE ROMANTIC NIGHT"

— WITH —

ROD LA ROCQUE CONRAD NAGLE

SPECIAL ADDED ALL-TALKING ATTRACTIONS

1930

Luxurious Apartments

TO LET

HADDON HALL APTS.

Renting Office: **Tel. Wilbank 4014**
2150 Sherbrooke St. W.

Only a few left of these ultra modern apartments—
4-5-6-7-11-14 rooms. Rents greatly reduced.

Frigidaire, Elevators, Open Fireplaces, etc.

Rent from $90.00

Will decorate to suit tenants.
Will furnish apartments if required.

Open Evenings and Sundays for Inspection.

1930

HEARTIEST NEW YEAR GREETINGS TO OUR PATRONS AND FRIENDS
MERCHANT TAILORED CLOTHES
Tailored clothes, with its fine material, workmanship and design are the soundest apparel investment you can make.
J. Shalinsky
LIMITED
TAILORS FOR MEN
761 ST. CATHERINE ST. WEST
Phone Lancaster 5558

1929

New Year Greetings to Our Many Friends and Patrons
For the Holidays
TEMPTING AND DELICIOUS
Sold Everywhere 50c a Pound
Kiddies and Mothers prefer them to others
GRANDMOTHER'S
CHOCOLATES
ONE POUND NET
CONFECTIONERS CO. LIMITED

DUTY OFF BRITISH GROWN TEA

"SALADA"

REDUCED PRICES

15c A POUND

BROWN LABEL (Black & Green) NOW 60c lb.
JAPAN GREEN TEA Price unchanged.
ALL OTHER LABELS Reduced 5c lb.

TO THE PUBLIC

THESE PRICES ARE EFFECTIVE NOW. DO NOT PAY MORE

Due to the action of the Government in abolishing the duty on British grown tea and to the lower costs of certain grades at the Tea Gardens, we are able to give the public the benefit of these substantial savings.

Unfortunately the market for finest teas has been advancing for some time so that we are only able to reduce our higher grades by 5c lb.

TO THE RETAIL GROCER

As always, we protect you against any los on SALADA TEA by making good to you the difference in the invoice value of your stock on hand. Please reduce prices at once at our expense. Claim form is being mailed to you at once.

SALADA TEA COMPANY OF CANADA, LIMITED

1930

GAYETY

HOME OF HIGH-CLASS BURLESQUE

TWICE DAILY - - 2.15 & 8.15 P.M.
SPECIAL MAT. DAILY - - 25c

WEEK BEGINNING SUNDAY EVE., DEC. 23rd.

THE DAWN OF A NEW ERA IN BURLESQUE ENTERTAINMENT!

NEW POLICY NEW IDEAS NEW INNOVATIONS
RUNWAY CHORUS OF SIXTEEN — FOUR SOUBRETTES

Opening Attraction

RUBE BERNSTEIN Presents His New Star

HINDA WASAU and her "HINDU BELLES"

With a Big Cast of Burlesque Favorites and a beauty chorus of

BEWITCHINGLY BEAUTIFUL "HINDU BELLES"

1928

WE EXTEND HEARTIEST NEW YEAR GREETINGS
TO OUR MANY FRIENDS AND PATRONS

BEFORE AFTER
or BETWEEN

THE HOURS
OF WORK

STILLICIOUS

Chocolate
Malted
Milk

The Miracle Food Drink
Created by Dairy Science

STILLICIOUS

will put driving power and steadiness in your work. Stillicious will give you the vigor of youth. Stillicious will create vitality. Stillicious is refreshing and a thirst quencher. Stillicious is palatable and does not contain carbonate water.

ALEXANDRA DAIRY LTD.

CHerrier 2872 MONTREAL

1929

1929

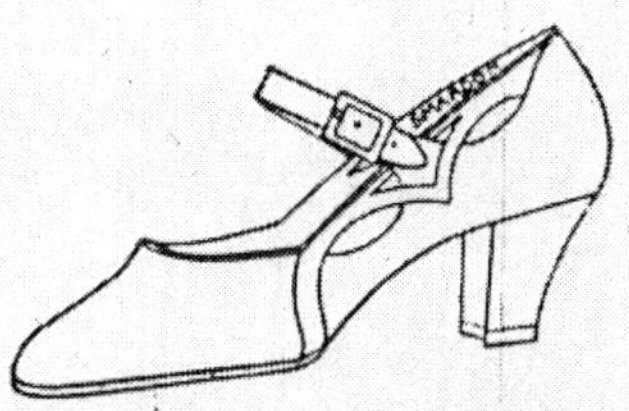

1928

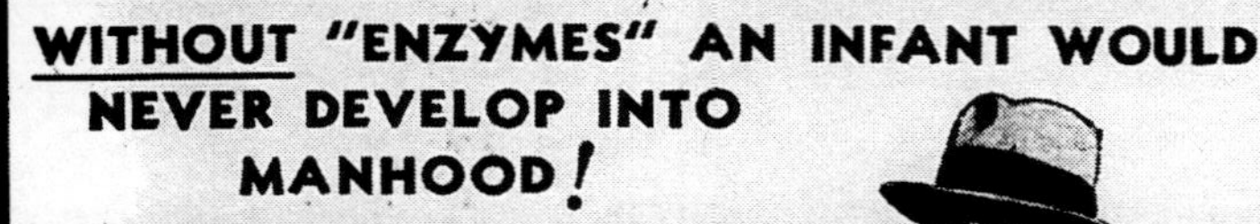

WITHOUT "ENZYMES" AN INFANT WOULD NEVER DEVELOP INTO MANHOOD!

אהן „ענזימס“ וואלט א קליין קינד זיך קיינמאל ניט ענטוויקעלט!

Dow Old Stock Ale

"ENZYMES" BUILD HEALTH

ענזימס

נעדיינקט או מיר פארקויפען

פוטער, קרים און קעז, פיטענטא און קרים קעז

אויך ספעשעל איין קרים פון פיור קרים

74 — פעירמאונט עווע. וועסט — 74

באשיינט אייער טיש מיט ריטשסטאון'ס ברויט

Richstones' Bakery Limited

RICHSTONE TRADE MARK REG.

Schoel Richstone Limited

Montreal Modern Business College

50.. St Lawrence Blvd. Telephone Dollard 9366

(Between St. Joseph Blvd. and Laurier Ave.)

אינדיווידועלער אונטערריכט

This article is from The Keneder Adler, April 1931, the bottom of p. 7

AFTERWORD

What is it like to live with an MHOH orphan?

From my experience, the home taught Myer Gordon gentleness, kindness, and generosity (with a smidgen of stubbornness—perhaps a survival technique?)—to a fault!

He feels that because he was so well cared for and loved, all people should experience those emotions, and he does his best. He goes out of his way, always, to help people, often sacrificing his own limited time and financial resources; for example, countless hours were spent on the phone to the city's Works Department, trying to get them to clean up an area of grass and pavement filled with dirty water and paper garbage—he felt it was a health hazard.

He is there for everybody! And he wakes up every morning *singing*!

He cherishes family and longs for a closeness that is not always there. He feels blessed to be living a comfortable life (with a loving wife), enjoys our home and his latest toy, one he did not have to make from old scraps—a computer!

He lacked material things as a child, and so has become a pack-rat, saving everything. "I've streetcar tickets older than you," he might say. Our garage has never had a car in it—it's so full of *stuff*! Not to mention his drawers in every room—a bonanza for flea-marketeers!

I have only one real complaint: I'm getting a bit tired of fighting with him over who should do the dishes (only one of the many *jobs* he seems to relish in his own home).

Selling Four Hundred Brothers and Sisters

You think it's easy? Writing a book is a whole lot easier than trying to sell it, let me tell you! But what an experience! The people you talk to and meet. The talking and talking, and phoning and phoning, and writing letters and letters, and travelling and travelling! Shyness has to fly out the window.

One action I took in my public relations letter-writing binge was to write George Cohon, the founder and senior chairman of McDonald's Canada. He had just written his own book, *From Russia with Fries*, and I had it, read it, and enjoyed it. What struck me were his stories of caring and helping people. So I wrote him a note of congratulations and mentioned that his book had many similarities to mine—and proceeded to tell him about *Four Hundred Brothers and Sisters.*

To my great surprise, a week later, his secretary phoned—he would like to buy our book! Which we promptly delivered. Recent phone calls to find out how or if he liked it—hoping for some printable comments—resulted in being told that he never made comments on books—he would have too many to handle! But, just the idea that George Cohon even wanted the book is exciting!

I've spoken many times with the two notable authors who wrote my original Forewords, Montreal's William Weintraub and Toronto's Morley Torgov. Two nicer gentlemen you could never meet. They have been full of advice (when asked), encouraging, and generous with their time. If you haven't already, do go out and buy their books—they deserve your patronage, and you deserve a splendid read!

So, the trick is to work 24/7, speak to the entire world, and try to enjoy every minute of it.

Montreal, Ottawa, and Toronto Jewish book fairs happily displayed our book. Myer, the orphan, and Judy, the author, have worked up an entertaining format. I read a bit from the book, and Myer talks about his home experiences. We've honed our talk and are told that we're not boring at all! For one read, which shall remain nameless (for obvious reasons), we were asked to cut our one-hour talk down to forty-five minutes, the sitting limit of our expected audience. We were so pleased to be told afterwards by the program director that she never saw anything like it—not only did we draw the biggest crowd for this type of program, but also, no one moved a muscle the entire time, and she detected emotion and teary eyes, which she had never seen before!

WOW for us!

And yes, we're always looking for a place to talk—have book, will travel, as it was once said. If we could limit our words to only five minutes, we'd have at least one TV gig, but what could we say in such a short time that would really be of value.

The story of the two Jewish orphanages in Montreal is starting to get better known, is becoming interesting to people interested in what happened in the community of their grandparents, parents, and even themselves—if they are in the eighties age-range. The expression, "I didn't know about that," is all too common and is followed by murmurs something like, "Gee, that's amazing, tell me more!" So we do! Life is not dull!

Four Hundred Brothers and Sisters (Book One) was the result of twelve years of alumni reunions and the need to put on paper the mostly unknown stories and history of the two orphanages—providing a vital link with Montreal's Jewish community of yesteryear.

Book Two contains more of everything—one for all people. It is simply a universal story of a community banding together to help the less fortunate in its midst.

And finally ...

A story is only as good as its readers' involvement in it. If it provides information with a touch of humour and educates in an enjoyable format, what more could a writer ask?

As I call it now—Book One—*Four Hundred Brothers and Sisters* initiated the beginnings of a story still widely unknown at the time. It seems to have touched the hearts and minds of its readers, such as Elaine Shapiro, program director, Cummings Jewish Seniors' Centre, Montreal, who wrote, "Your book has made an impact on me ... it brought to light and fleshed out a part of my grandmother's life, of which I had only heard fragments. Her name was Pearl Rosenstein and she was a board member at the orphanage. My parents and grandparents died early in my life, so I have very little history and I therefore treasure any little pieces of the puzzle I can get! For others, the book has enriched their sense of Montreal Jewish history and their place in it! So on their behalf and on mine, I applaud you and thank you for the way in which you have touched all of our lives!"

And, Margaret Goldik, co-editor of the *Montreal Review of Books*, wrote in the Fall/Winter 2003 issue, "The meat of the book is to be found in the stories of the men and women who were once residents of the MHOH. They reminisce not only about their years there, but also tell what they have done with the rest of their lives. With an association of *alumni*, a newsletter, and reunions, the *brothers and sisters* are still looking out for each other."

This book—Book Two—wraps up the history and includes engaging anecdotes from alumni and families of the volunteers *of old*, illustrating it all with photos from the past. Yours to enjoy now.

—Judy Gordon

APPENDIX A

Toronto's Orphanage

Arthur Daniel Hart, in *The Jew in Canada*, 1926, wrote about Toronto's orphanage. Like the two in Montreal, this important facility was mostly unknown—except to the many wonderful volunteers who ran it. This is its history until 1926.

> On September 15, 1909, a meeting of the Toronto Ladies' Aid Society was held to consider the case of a Jewish widow unable to support herself and her two children. Prior to this time, any Jewish children in such circumstances had to be taken care of at Christian institutions. At the meeting referred to, amongst others, the following ladies were present: Mrs. Norman Helpert, Mrs. Rafelman, Mrs. I. Cooper, Mrs. B. Cooper, Mrs. M. Cohen, the late Mrs. N. Smith, the late Mrs. A. Landsberg, and Mrs. M. Kaplan, also the Rev. Mr. Kaplan.
>
> It was decided to rent a house on the corner of Elizabeth and Dundas streets. The widow already mentioned was appointed the first superintendent, and the children of poor working mothers, who had no one to look after them during the day, were taken care of here during their parents' absence at work. The house was equipped as a nursery, with a dispensary on the lower floor; a soup kitchen was also operated. Different ladies came in to supervise, and the late Mrs. A. Landsberg, who in her lifetime was one of the most zealous workers, was in charge of the *investigation*. Thus was started the first Jewish orphanage in Toronto, with Mrs. I. Cooper as its first president.
>
> The premises on Elizabeth Street were occupied for about a year, and not being equal to the requirements, the orphanage moved to a building on Simcoe Street ... at that time purchased by the United Charities. At first only the top floor of this building was needed to fill the requirements of the orphanage, but

later the demands for space increased to such an extent, that the whole building was occupied, and the orphanage remained in these premises for fourteen years.

In 1921, Miss Rose Levy assumed the superintendency, and one of the first changes she made was in changing the name to the Jewish Children's Home, and the institution has been called this ever since.

A notable day in the history of the home was reached in 1922, when the old stand in Simcoe Street was exchanged for a beautiful residence on Annette Street, where there may be found a happy family of over twenty children. Although the building may accommodate thirty-five, there are seldom that many in residence. The home, after all, is mainly a clearing house, for the management strongly believes in re-establishing families or in securing foster homes for the children, when that is impossible.

The structure on Annette Street contains twenty rooms, which have been converted into dormitories for the children, and pleasant reception, writing, study and dining rooms, kitchen, laundry, sewing room, etc. There is also a dispensary in which are closets that contain all kinds of medicine and other requirements for first aid for the children.

Children of school age pursue their education at the nearby schools, and care is taken to have all present at a Jewish Sunday school every week, when they are instructed in the religion of their fathers. The Sisterhood of Bond Street Synagogue has undertaken to see that the children attend Sunday school all year and supply the price of transportation to and from the synagogue. The boys attend Chedar [daily]. Several children are taught music by voluntary teachers, and those who wish are instructed in sewing and dancing. The girls have also formed a Brownie pack. The children ... make their own beds, help with the dusting and dishes and with the sorting of linens. The older boys help in the grounds ... [go to] Edmund Scheuer for the religious instruction that he gives the children over the week, and they also look for their Saturday afternoon treat of fruit, from the same gentleman. The children also await the Friday night dish of ice cream, which is always furnished them by Mrs. D. Dunkelman.

The superintendent, Rose Levy, is a graduate nurse and another of her first moves was to have each child call her "Aunt Rose." Like all wise disciplinarians, Miss Levy imposes very few rules. She emphasizes the fact that the house belongs to the young people, and sees to it that they feel at home in every part. Blessed with an inborn love of little folk, she resents anything that would draw attention to the misfortunes of her charges, and is determined to so [run] her home that sunshine, and not shadow, should envelop their lives. In her own private room, Miss Levy has placed an extra bed for the convenience of any sick boy or girl, and is thus able to bring many a child through a light illness. The staff also consists of a nurse, maid, cook, janitor, gardener, and laundress.

The expenses of the home are borne by the Federation of Jewish Philanthropies, and the home is also in receipt of a municipal grant. Most of the furniture has been donated, and some of the rooms have been entirely equipped, among the donors being the following: Eastern Star, Lions' Club, Boot and Shoe Society, Mr. Silverman (stocking darner), Mr. and Mrs. M. Kohan (Blue Room), Mrs. I. Helpert (entire room), Senior Council of Jewish Women (entire room), Mrs. M. L. Willinsky, Mrs. B. Wise, Mrs. Norman Helpert, Mrs. M. Mehr, Mrs. A. Landsberg, and others.

Mrs. S. Greenfarb was president of the home for six years, from 1918 to 1924, when she resigned, and much credit is due her for her indefatigable work. The following are the present officers: Rev. Mr. Kaplan, honorary president; Mrs. M. Mehr, president; Mrs. M. Kaplan, 1st vice-president; Mrs. L. Bert, 2nd vice-president; Mrs. I. Cohen, 3rd vice-president; Miss Meta Rotenberg, secretary-treasurer; Mrs. L. Adelberg, treasurer; Mrs. H. James, recording secretary; Mrs. F. Hutner, corresponding secretary. The following are the convenors: Mrs. M. L. Willinsky, House Committee; Mrs. D. Stein, Sewing Committee; Mrs. N. Rosenberg, Ways & Means Committee; and Mrs. D. Wise, Investigating Committee.

Many friends contribute to the happiness of the children, and the Sunnyside Lodge, I.O.O.F., the I.O.B.B., the Shriners, and the Patriotic Association have given them delightful days in the country. Whenever any kind of transportation is required to move children to any place, Mr. Harry Rosenthal has always been ready and willing to furnish it, and he is regarded as one of the staunchest friends of the institution.

At least once a month, and generally more frequently, Dr. David Perlman and Dr. I. R. Smith visit the home to inspect the children, and at any time physicians willingly respond to a call for professional advice. Each child must be examined by Dr. Perlman and granted a certificate before admission to the home.

Much of the success of the home is due to splendid and complete co-operation between the superintendent and the Board of Management, and the support of the Federation of Jewish Philanthropies.

An addition to the present building is in course of construction, and when completed, the Jewish Children's Home will be one of the most attractive and perfectly equipped establishments of Toronto.

According to the Ontario Jewish Archives, the home closed in 1933, but served as temporary and emergency housing to about forty children while they waited to be moved into foster homes, under the jurisdiction of the Jewish Children's Bureau. The building itself was closed in 1936.

More details can be found in Dr. Stephen Speisman's book, written in 1979, *The Jews of Toronto: A History to 1937.*

APPENDIX B

Winnipeg's Orphanages

To keep the history of the orphanages together, this information, by A. D. Hart in *The Jew in Canada*, 1926, is excerpted here.

> Prior to April 1912, Jewish children who were left orphans and dependent upon the public were placed in non-Jewish homes or institutions. With the Jewish population of Winnipeg and Western Canada growing larger ... a foregone conclusion that such a condition would not long be allowed to remain ... led to the inauguration of a Jewish orphanage for the purpose not only of feeding and housing these unfortunate dependants, but also of educating them and bringing them up in the faith of their forefathers.
>
> The Hebrew Ladies' Orphan Home Association (later the Ladies' Society of the Jewish Orphanage) was formed in 1912 to establish a Jewish Orphans' Home ... the local B'nai B'rith lodge also took the matter up. The first concrete step was taken when representatives of both groups met in September 1912.
>
> Chairman R. S. Robinson offered a substantial sum of money toward the proposed project on the condition the institution bear the name of his mother, Esther Robinson.
>
> On July 25, 1913, the Canadian Jewish Orphanage came into existence, with Mr. A. H. Aronovitch as president. At the same time, two houses were purchased on Robinson Street to be run by a group of men for a similar purpose and to be known as the Esther Robinson Orphans' Home—leading ultimately to the establishment of a new orphanage, old folks' home, and Jewish hospital.
>
> The outbreak of the Great War the following year put a halt to such a plan. Then, too, there was a growing feeling amongst the general community that there was no need nor reason for two orphan homes under separate management and roofs, with

the same objectives, serving the same purpose, and both appealing to the same public for assistance and support.

Negotiations were initiated with the Esther Robinson Home with a view to amalgamation ... By October 14, 1916, a *get-together* decision was reached. On February 5, 1917, Mr. E. R. Levinson was elected president of the joint home.

The first important task was to find a qualified superintendent. Assisted by the Independent Order of B'nai B'rith at Chicago, the committee selected Mr. I. L. Greenberg, then assistant superintendent of a Jewish home in Chicago. Both Mr. and Mrs. Greenberg had been actively engaged in similar work in New York as well as Chicago. In April 1917, they came to Winnipeg as superintendent and matron.

Mr. Greenberg's advanced ideas on child care were new to the Jewish public, even to the directors themselves. But a sufficient number were ready and willing to cooperate. It was decided to mount, in Western Canada, the biggest fundraising campaign in the history of Canadian Jewry—to raise $100,000 for a new home. By September 1918, 1,500 workers had raised $40,000 in cash and $40,000 in pledges.

Plans from United States orphans' homes were incorporated, ensuring the latest improvements and design to meet the needs and requirements of the children. The laying of the cornerstone took place on August 10, 1919, the stone being laid by the late Ekiel Bronfman. The official opening and transfer of children to their new home took place in February 1920.

In 1921, Mr. Alan Bronfman, a young barrister new to the city, was elected president at the age of twenty-five. The home, facing a serious financial depression, required young blood and energy.

Building and Grounds

The magnificent new Jewish Orphans' Home cost well over $125,000 and provides for about one hundred children. It stands on five and one-half acres of park-like grounds, surrounded by a grove of beautiful trees. Part of this furnishes vegetables of every description throughout the summer ... enough to store and last all winter. (See photos in Early Archival photo section)

The Tudor-style resembles a large private home ... structurally fireproof throughout, floors of reinforced concrete with hollow tile walls and partitions, and staircases leading directly outside. There are marble floors almost everywhere.

Separate entrances for boys and girls at the rear of the building lead directly to their playrooms, living rooms, and dormitories on their respective floors, and if necessary or desired, the sexes can be kept entirely apart in separate wings—with their own bathrooms and lavatories.

The accommodation design allows for every detail—closets, baths, and individual basins at different heights for the varying size of the children, plus linen and locker rooms for each wing. The matron's rooms, next to the dormitories, have overlooking casement windows for closer supervision of the sleeping quarters.

An isolation hospital with separate access on the main floor provides a clinic. Nearby are quarters for the superintendent, an office, boardroom, library, study, dining room, and kitchen. In the basement are playrooms, classrooms, lavatories, and showers, as well as refrigerating departments and an electrically equipped laundry. On the third floor is a large assembly hall for social and convention purposes.

Jewish Winnipeg and Western Canada from Fort William to Vancouver responded generously with financial support; on March 18, 1923, the president reported that the home was clear of debt, the first Jewish institution in Winnipeg and Western Canada to claim its land, building, furnishings, and equipment as its own—no interest, no tax arrears.

Activities of the Children at the Home

The children are so busy that they do not have much time on their hands. Every week sees new activities ... the home is constantly kept in the public eye: huge carnivals, dramatic presentations by the kids, and performances by the children's choir and band. Any child who has a special talent for a particular instrument, such as the violin or piano, is given special instruction; the home can boast of at least one child composer, a girl of fourteen, whose remarkable selections are played by the band of which she is a member.

Two teachers, under the guidance of the superintendent, himself a Hebrew scholar of high merit, and a special education committee, give the children modern schooling in the Hebrew language and on the principles of the Jewish religion and Jewish national aspirations. Older boys pray every morning with tefillin, and services are held in the third floor synagogue every Friday night, Saturday morning, and on holidays, and can also attract as many as two hundred people from the city and the country. Their forty-two-voice children's choir participates and is in great demand for concerts and other entertainments. This education of the children in their Biblical history, daily prayers, the grace, which they say before and after meals, and the strict dietary laws, which are observed, all serve to create in the home a thoroughly Jewish atmosphere.

The boys help in many ways; useful and reliable, they take a special interest in the garden. Girls are taught the practical duties of cooking, serving, and general housekeeping ... how to sew, mend, wash and dry dishes, set and clear a table, prepare a meal, wash and iron a dress, and make a bed. The fully equipped playgrounds permit tennis, football, and baseball games in summer, skating and hockey matches in winter. There are numerous picnics, entertainments, and social functions. They enjoy club meetings and storytelling and a splendid library with hundreds of volumes of general literature, magazines, and periodicals, their reading supervised strictly by the superintendent so that "it is pursued along proper lines."

The children are taught the value of thrift by the encouragement of individual savings accounts and other methods of competition and awards.

They are healthy, a tribute to their clean, bright surroundings, and to the devotion and care by the superintendent and his wife, whose whole aim is to make the home a real family home. It is a tribute also to the devotion of the Jewish medical men, whose regular inspections minister to the eyes, ears, throats, and teeth of the children, and who look after them promptly and efficiently without remuneration.

The number of children grows each year, until today over 110 are cared for. Consulted as to their desires or leanings, some children are given business courses, or, if of "a scholarly bent," are given an opportunity for higher education. When they leave the home, an after-care committee keeps in constant touch with them, lending assistance and advice where necessary.

The home is open to the general public at all times. A prominent part continues to be played by the Jewish communities of Western Canada ... The Jewish Orphanage receives from the federal budget an allowance for maintenance of the Winnipeg quota of children in the home, as well as those who come from outside Winnipeg, while the work of the Women's Auxiliary is the veritable backbone of the home.

APPENDIX C

Alumni Lists

To the best of our knowledge, the following lists are complete. Women are listed by their maiden names with their married names in parentheses.

Montreal Home Alumni

Albert, Henry
Albert, Julius
Alper, Max
Alper, Nat
Avrith, Michael
Avrith, Nettie (Shragie)
Baker, Harry
Berman, Ann (Alexander)
Berman, Sam
Bye, Abe
Bye, Edie
Chart, Ruth (Littlefield)
Cohen, Herbie
Cohen, Manny
Cohen, Nathan
Cohen, Yetta (Novak)
Dick, Lester
Epstein, Sally Ann (Kerman)
Fishman, Lionel
Fishman, Muriel
Fishman, Ruth (Tobin)
Florian, Sam
Freedman, Sam
Goldsmith, Bessie (Grossner)
Goldsmith, Nathan
Gordon, Martin
Gottlieb, Eva (Goldberg)
Greene, Harry
Israel, Harvey
Israel, Shirley (Thau)
Kushner, Alex
Lang, Lou
Lieberman, Michael
Lipson, David
Matt, Hilda (Brownstone)
Matt, Max
Melnick, Martin
Miller, Jack
Nachbar, Mildred (n/a)
Palmer, Aaron
Pfeffer, Irving
Randolph, Moss
Reider, Josephine (Justitz)
Reisler, Annie (Thomas)
Reisler, Reuben
Sandell, Joseph
Savitsky, Reva (Schuman)
Savitsky, Sylvia (Rasminsky)

Schwartz, Harry
Schwartz, Libby (Kashenberg)
Schwartz, Samuel
Smilovitch, Ruth (Furman)
Soloman, Aaron (Abie Schmoiser)
Spielman, Sara (Frenkel)
Stolov, Ben*
Stolov, Judith (Kazdan)
Stolov, Matthew*
Stolov, Meyer
Turowitz, Allan
Turowitz, Jerry
Wener, Ella (Wilbourne)
Yanovitch, Vivienne (Urman)
Zimmerman, Sylvia (Sherry Grossman)
Zukerman, Jack

* Ben and Matthew Stolov were not placed with Judith and Meyer—they were put in the Julius Richardson Convalescent Hospital in Châteauguay.

(Coincidentally, Judy Gordon was instrumental in a fundraiser for the new J. R. Hospital, which opened on Côte-Saint-Luc Road in N.D.G. in the 1950s. She organized a school concert, charging ten cents per student, and donated all proceeds—$150—to the construction of the facility.)

Montefiore Home Alumni

Adelstein, Minnie (Leibo)
Adelstein, Moe
Bercusson, Sara (Connie Gore)
Cherry, Dave
Frankel, Hymie
Frankel, Ruth (Margolcse)
Garber, Ben
Gordon, Myer
Greenberg, Earl
Greenberg, Helen (Zawalsky)
Label,Willie
Letnick, Morris
Mayoff, Saul
Miretsky, Edith (Landen)
Miretsky, Gert (Golub)
Miretsky, Ruth (Gorelik)
Naiman, Teddy
Newton, Jeannie (Lichtenstein)
Rasminsky, Sam
Schwartz, Hymie
Senderoff, Abe
Senderoff, Jack
Shamovitch, Issac (Shamai)
Shein, Vita (Seidler)
Sheiner, Albert (Abie)
Sheiner, Dr. Sydney (Shaner)
Sklar, Ida (Lewis)
Steinberg, Issie
Ticker, Moe
Ticker, Sydney
Tolmasky, Claire (Margolian)
Tolmasky, Saul

Wagon, Anita (Bercovitch)
White, Saul

MHOH Alumni Who Have Passed Away

The year is listed where known.

Prior to 1992

Aaron, Billy
Appel, Frances
Axman, Charlie (1990)
Baker, Frankie
Baker, Johnnie
Belkin, Ralph
Bercovitch, Rosie (Kaufman)
Black, Oscar
Black, Seymour (1975)
Bloom, Charlie
Broitman, Surie
Brumer, Ben (1991)
Brumer, Harry
Brumer, Hymie
Brumer, Sam
Burke, Max
Bydoff, Norman
Bye, M/M Henry Bye
Chart, Issie
Cherry, Rose (Abrams)
Cohen, Josephine (Romisher)
Cohen, Lynn
Cohen, Moishe
Davies, Charlie
Engel, Miriam
Epstein, Philip
Feldman, Lily (Braverman)
Feldman, Sam
Fine, Hymie
Freedman, Issie
Gold, Esther (Mann)
Gold, Jennie
Goldstein, Dora (Sheiner)
Gordon, Ben (1987)
Greenberg, Ann (Gluzman)
Greenberg, Joe
Harris, Bernard
Jacobson, Ann (Aaronson)
Kaminsky, Harry
Kantor, Mary
Kramer, Milton
Kravitz, Solly
Lenetsky, Eli
Levenson, Irving
Markson, Leon
Mendelson, Mike (1992)
Miller, Eli (1985)
Milstein, Dave
Milstein, Fanny
Milstein, Max
Milstein, Saul
Muchnick, Bessie
Muchnick, Oscar
Ogulnick, Dr. Maurice
Ostrovsky, Louis
Plotnick, Oscar
Raffalovitch, Mendel
Raven, Lou (1990)
Rosenberg, Mollie
Roth, Oscar

Rubin, Mollie
Rubin, Sollie
Schacter, Dave
Schalek, Arthur
Shano, Evelyn (Furlong) (1992)
Shein, Abie
Sokoloff, Abie
Sokoloff, Phyllis (Felicia Sotell) (1992)
Sokoloff, Jack
Sokoloff, Mary
Spielman, Eddie
Spielman, Nathan (1988)
Spinner, Jack
Steinberg, Issie
Stoffmaker, Avrum
Umansky, Sarah (Gatis)
Velter, Goldie
Velter, Tillie
Vineberg, Maurice
Wener, Leah
Wener, Sara
Wiseman, Ben (1992)
Wyne, Hilda (Benjamin) (1990)
Zitser, Samuel (1927)

1993-1998

Frankel, Toby
Golub, Arnold
Gross, Dr. Jack
Greene, Arnold
Hoffman, Caroline (Silverman)
Jacobson, Jack
Kaufman, Sam
Kramer, Richard
Lenetsky, Harry
Miretsky, Joe
Morganstein, Willie
Rasminsky, Herbie
Schwartz, Leo
Smilovitch, Doris
Stotland, Sam
Turowitz, Bernard
Wyne, Ida (Shulman) (1997)
Wyne, Nancy (Ogilvy) (1998)
Wyne, Simmie
Zukerman, Morris (1998)

1999-2004

Albert, Leo (2000)
Baker, Sam
Berman, Charles (2002)
Bloom, Louis
Bloom, Willie
Brownston, John
Brumer, Louis
Cherry, Harry
Dubin, Celia (Altrows) (2004)
Feldman, Sophie (Kazdan)
Greenberg, Harry
Harris, Jake (2002)
Hoffman, Tillie (Simon) (2002)
Jacobson, Hymie (1999)
Levy, Lionel (2002)
Lewis, Solly (2003)
Miller, Harry (2002)
Miller, Joe (2000)
Miller, Loretta (Rodman) (2000)
Miller, Moishe (2002)

Ostroff, Harry (2002)
Rosenberg, Eddie
Senderoff, Jesse (Lieber) (2000)
Shapiro, Joe (2004)
Shenker, Ann (Hershon)
Simon, Morris (2001)
Sklar, Yetta (Chazenoff)
Smilovitch, Solly (2000)
Ticker, Shirley (Broitman) (2003)
Tolmasky, Abe
Wiseman, Celia (Tina Rosen) (2002)
Yanovitch, Cecil (Young) (2001)

ACKNOWLEDGEMENTS

Thank you to

- Andrea Lemieux, editor extraordinaire, for her valued comments and changes;
- Sue Bronson, architect, chair of Mile End Memories, Montreal;
- Janice Rosen, director, Archives, Canadian Jewish Congress (CJC) National Archives, Montreal

for their time, patience, support, additional material, and mostly for their interest in seeing that Book #2 is printed.

- Rebecca Margolis, Montreal, for her Yiddish translation of four articles from the 1931 *Keneder Adler*, and
- Miriam Beckerman, Toronto, for her informal translation of same.
- Joan & Hershel Pesner, Montreal, my 'newly-found cousins', whose enthusiasm helped us spread this important piece of Montreal history to Montreal's Jewish community.
- Sholom Aleichem, *Adventures of Mottel The Cantor's Son,* (in two parts) translated by Tamara Kahana. Part one: *In Kasrilovka: Hoorah, I'm an Orphan*! The children of Sholom Aleichem and Henry Schuman Inc., New York:1953
- Sue Bronson, Montefiore Hebrew Orphans' Home—notes, August 27, 2002
- Abe Cohen, *Canadian Jewish Chronicle*, April 28, 1916, *Our Orphans' Home,* pp. 1 and 13
- Janice Rosen, article in the CJC National Archives newsletter of 1946, based on the minute books of the Montreal Hebrew Sheltering and Orphans' Home from 1914 to 1922
- Joe Fiorito, *Toronto Star* columnist, September 2003
- Leslie Lutsky, producer *"Jewish Digest"* on Radio Centre-Ville, for being our *self-professed* groupie
- *Montreal Gazette* reporter Ann McLaughlin,1990, reunion article
- John Kalbfleisch, columnist for the *Gazette*, Montreal, the story of anti-Semitism at Aberdeen School—from 1919.

We greatly appreciate the support of the following:

Benefactor

Judge Irving and Marilyn Pfeffer, San Fransisco (MHOH)

Patrons

Harry Baker, Montreal (MHOH)
Sandy and Norman Burns, Toronto
Lola and Larry Caplan, Toronto
Ben Garber, Montreal (MHOH)
Eileen and Dave Ginberg, Florida
Edie and Sonny Goldstein, Toronto
Martin Gordon, Laval, PQ (MHOH)
Myer and Judy Gordon, Toronto (MHOH)
Sylvia and Moe Greenspoon, Toronto
Sherry and Dr. Ivan Grossman, Los Altos, California (MHOH)
Mary Hoffman, Montreal
Aurora and Peter Kashkarian, Toronto
Marie Claire and Moe Letnick, White Rock, British Columbia (MHOH)
Ida Sklar Lewis, Montreal (MHOH)
Barbara Linetsky, Mississauga, Ontario (father in MHOH)
Wanda and Max Matt, Bloomfield, Connecticut (MHOH supervisor)
Phyllis and Mike Mendell, Montreal
Aaron Palmer, Kingston, Ontario
Connie Rosen, Montreal—"in memory of my late mother Tina Rosen (MHOH)"
Leonard Rosen, Montreal—"in memory of my late wife Tina Rosen"
Claire and Sam Schwartz, Florida (MHOH)
Nettie and Al Shragie, Montreal (MHOH)
Upper Canada Lodge, #1615, B'nai Brith Canada, Toronto
Sally and Dr. Gerald Weisbrod, Toronto

Supporters

Frances and Henry Albert, Montreal (MHOH)
Max Alper, Montreal (MHOH)

Kathy and Steve Asch, Brechin, Ontario
Stephen Chappell, Napanee, Ontario
June and Herb Cohen, Montreal (MHOH)
Irma and Lester Dick, Kirkland, Quebec (MHOH)
Warren Dick, Montreal
Muriel Fishman, Montreal (MHOH)
Sandy and Earl Greenberg, Toronto (MHOH)
Alvin J. Guttman, Montreal
Gloria and Cyril Houser, Toronto
Edward Kogut, Toronto
Min and Hy Leibovitch (Leibo), Edmonton, Alberta (MHOH)
Iris and Jack Lieber, Toronto
Burtha and Henry Liss, Toronto
Leslie Lutsky, Montreal
Karen and Sam Mathewson, Toronto
Shirley and Ted Naiman, Montreal (MHOH)
Evelyn Rabkin, Toronto
Vita and Eric Seidler, Toronto (MHOH)
Jerry Shapiro, Toronto
Morley Slover, Ottawa
Dorothy and Aaron (Schmoiser) Soloman, Florida (MHOH)
Bill and Beth Stern, Toronto
Shirley Thau, Montreal (MHOH)
Devra and Alvin Wegler, Thornhill, Ontario
Dorothy and Saul White, Montreal (MHOH)
Eleanor Wynston, Aurora, Ontario
Louise and Gordon Zakaib, Montreal
Jack Zukerman, Montreal (MHOH)

INDEX

Every effort has been made; however, all spellings of names could not be verified—spellings that are in doubt are in brackets.

About the Book

More Response to *Four Hundred Brothers and Sisters*

"You've done a remarkable job ... in bringing this story to life. Because we live just below the little pole at 455 Claremont, the former orphanage is just five houses up from us on the opposite side of the street. It's now a retirement home for Catholic nuns and priests."

Professor Myron Echenberg,
History Department, McGill University, Montreal

"The author ... has done an impressive amount of research for her absorbing and ... entertaining account of bygone days ... There is plenty here to interest anyone curious about a unique chapter in Canadian Jewish life during a period of change and painful acculturation."

Rabbi Bernard Baskin, Hamilton

"You wrote a book which sheds light on an all but a forgotten chapter in Canadian Jewish history, which is now available to the public ... What's important is that Myer's story, and those of the other orphans, is out there circulating in the world ... The fact that the orphanages will be remembered because of your book is the biggest reward any writer could ask for."

Rafi Aaron, Toronto poet-author

"A great book and accomplishment. You should be very proud."

Dr. Steve Freidberg, Head of Neurology, Leahy Clinic, Boston